Ken Yeang

Eco Skyscrapers: Volume 2

Ken Yeang

Eco Skyscrapers: Volume 2

Lucy Bullivant

images
Publishing

Published in Australia in 2011 by
The Images Publishing Group Pty Ltd
ABN 89 059 734 431
6 Bastow Place, Mulgrave, Victoria 3170, Australia
Tel: +61 3 9561 5544 Fax: +61 3 9561 4860
books@imagespublishing.com
www.imagespublishing.com

1006381777

National Library of Australia Cataloguing-in-Publication entry:

Author:	Yeang, Ken, 1948-
Title:	Eco skyscrapers Volume 2 / by Ken Yeang, edited by Lucy Bullivant.
Edition:	1st ed.
ISBN:	9781864703870 (hbk.)
Subjects:	Skyscrapers.
	Skyscrapers--Designs and plans.
	Architecture and climate.
	Architecture and energy conservation.
	Architecture--Environmental aspects.
Other Authors/Contributors: Bullivant, Lucy.	
Dewey Number:	720.483

Coordinating editor: Debbie Fry

Digital production and printing by Everbest Printing Co. Ltd., in Hong Kong/China, printed on 140 gsm Gold East Matt Art

IMAGES has included on its website a page for special notices in relation to this and our other publications.
Please visit www.imagespublishing.com.

Contact

T. R. Hamzah & Yeang Sdn. Bhd.
No. 8 Jalan Satu
Taman Sri Ukay
68000 Ampang
Selangor, Malaysia
[Tel] +603 4257 1966 [Fax] +603 4256 1005
[Email] trhy@trhamzahyeang.com

Llewelyn Davies Yeang
Brook House
Torrington Place
London WC1E 7HN UK
[Tel] +44 020 7637 0181 [Fax] +44 020 7637 8740
[Email] info@ldavies.com

Websites
www.trhamzahyeang.com
www.ldavies.com

Contents

Ken Yeang's Green Genres of Architecture
by Lucy Bullivant

Ecologically advanced architecture requires far more than the green certification, ecoengineering gadgetry, carbon profiling and building performance simulation studies that many green design practitioners habitually apply. The public's growing green consciousness is certainly now matched in architectural practice by extensive applications of sustainable design criteria and measures. It seems, though, that the expanding range of green 'bottom-up' community initiatives, in recycling for example, across the world are not yet reflected by sufficient innovation in green buildings by architects. Ken Yeang, a Malaysian architect and world expert in ecological architecture, is undeniably one specialist who has worked to bring about a paradigm shift in green design and the application of its ideas, theory and techniques to the design and planning of cities and buildings—including the tall building type.

Yeang has designed and built a large number of low-energy green buildings, including several high-rises, in over 20 countries worldwide during his 35 years of practice. Each project he undertakes gives him the opportunity to build upon his earlier ideas and to evolve several ecological architectural features: the bioclimatic skyscraper, the concept of ecoinfrastructure, the idea of vertical landscaping, the ecobridge and the ecocell. His key philosophy is simply that architecture and its relationship to society has to be as integrated as its ecological relationship to the natural environment. The challenge he sets himself, which he continues to live by, is to design our built environments as artificial ecosystems that are seamlessly and benignly biointegrated with the natural environment.

In the face of widespread lack of awareness within the industry when he began practicing in the mid 1970s, Yeang has consistently maintained that a bioclimatic approach is the best initial design strategy, delivering at the outset a low-energy and critically regionalist design. The design responds in a number of ways to local climatic factors that vary depending on a site's location and latitude. These factors shape and configure the built form and orientation, and enable Yeang to design its architectural component systems. These climate-related strategies optimise the ambient energies of specific locations, taking into account local meteorological conditions and seasonal variations.

Yeang points out that bioclimatic design is 'not to be mistaken as green design in its entirety, but simply as one aspect of green design'. Bioclimatic design results in a passive-mode, low-energy built form—it is therefore such an excellent starting point for green design that it is an obvious initial strategy. The logic of bioclimatic design drove much of Yeang's early work. He argues that bioclimatic design is superior to other solutions, one reason being that it remains effective in the event of power failures. It also provides a 'scaffold' for subsequent energy-saving enhancements, for example the adoption of mixed-mode systems and other full-mode automated energy-saving systems and productive systems.

Yeang's first benchmark project was his own house—the Roof-Roof House—completed in 1985. This provided his first opportunity to break the mould in terms of both design and technology. He undertook a number of experiments in the design that promoted conventional bioclimatic design: in line with its name, there is a double louvred roof to keep the building and spaces below cool; a swimming pool serves as an evaporative-cooling device for the adjoining living spaces; and wind walls between the building and its boundary walls drive wind into the ground floor interiors to provide cooling and cross ventilation.

One of Yeang's most recent buildings is the 15-storey Solaris (see page 42) in the Fusionopolis research and business park of Singapore's pioneering one-north district (the masterplan of which was prepared by Zaha Hadid Architects). Solaris is a world-leading example of a building that has landscaping entwined throughout the built form. With over 8000 square metres of landscaping within the built form, the greening exceeds the area of the site by 13%. This is an innovation for which Yeang has received much acclaim—his seamless and benign biointegration of building with landscape, both horizontally and vertically, is a prominent aspect of his work.

Yeang has combined architecture and the environment in this way more than any other architect. He is meticulous in ensuring that each scheme is also advanced in its ecological identity and performance. Two tower blocks in Solaris are separated by a large, naturally-ventilated central atrium with automated operable glass louvres overhead and novel rain-screen walls that are spanned by a series of sky bridges connecting the office floors. A continuous, 1.5-kilometre landscaped spiral ramp—that is in effect a vertical 'linear park'—connects an escalating sequence of roof gardens with corner sky terraces that interpenetrate the building's façade. Combined with a solar-shaft cut through the upper floors of the second block are sensor-driven lighting, natural ventilation, extensive sun-shading louvres and a rainwater harvesting system. The design has been awarded the Singapore Building Control Authority's (BCA) GreenMark Platinum rating, Singapore's top sustainable building accreditation.

As clients now turn to sustainable solutions, green design becomes increasingly part of mainstream thinking with the identity of green buildings also rising as a priority. What should a green building look like? Yeang's response is to create a built form as a vertical landscape. This is a strong theme in Yeang's buildings, which vary in their range of green strategies according to brief and context. Yeang's focus on green infrastructure as well as other sustainable elements sets him apart from other green architects. He believes architecture is a variable craft that is predicated on the basis of positive and restorative planning measures 'that will contribute beneficially to the ecosystems'. He contends that design as ecomimicry has the potential to provide the designer with inspiration for inventive models derived from the properties, processes and structure of ecosystems. However, a pitfall of many architects' work is that they engage in ecomimicry in aesthetic and superficial ways only. Yeang steers away from this visual mimicry alone, because it is easy to copy a natural form at the expense of other considerations.

He feels strongly that an ecologically advanced built form should have its own aesthetic, something sociologist Richard Sennett agrees with. 'Environmental problems should be a stimulus to innovative design. The architect should think more like a Roman designing an aqueduct. Instead of the inherent notion that ecodesign should be self-effacing, it should be dramatised', he commented at The Urban Age South America conference in São Paulo in December 2009. During a session at the same event, Mexican architect Enrique Norten concurred: 'We are starting to understand that this knowledge can create new forms of urban space'. For an architect to work like a technician is not enough. Neither green building nor sustainable environmental design are fixed ideals, but rather are evolving concepts to be refined and reassessed with each new project.

Can a tall building be green? This is a question that Yeang's work has addressed since the early years of the 21st century. In this time, he has designed a new genre of bioclimatic skyscrapers that have drawn worldwide attention. He contests the widespread assumption that tall buildings as a built form are inherently energy-inefficient and harmful to the environment. Yeang's skyscrapers are iconic, and all deviate in major ways from conventional towers. Yeang does something no other major architect of his generation does: he applies bioclimatic design principles to the high-rise built form and, at the same time, combines the inorganic hard (buildings) and the organic soft (landscape) in a masterful way throughout the entire structure. Internally, Yeang often applies a wide range of green and bioclimatic strategies including evaporative cooling walls, wing walls for natural ventilation and ecocells, which bring vegetation, daylight and natural ventilation into basement areas.

The Spire Edge Tower in Manesar, Gurgaon, India serves as a metaphor for the ability of humankind to protect and interact with nature through benign applications of green technologies and landscaping. It has a vertical ecoinfrastructure that utilises a combination of ecological terraces and ecowalls that start from the centre of the ground level IT park and continue up through green ramps to the top of the building and then back down again via a ramp on the other face of the tower. This highly visual concept can only function if the vegetation is well maintained. Yeang is proud to bring green elements to the forefront of his designs—he does not hide them away as do many other architects who take an engineering-driven approach to ecological architecture. Conspicuous green lung spaces in the form of landscaped garden terraces are combined with passive energy and other ecologically advanced systems in the Spire Edge Tower.

Yeang was one of the first architects to use sky gardens and green roofs extensively in skyscrapers. These innovations have now become common, especially in Singapore after the completion of the National Library in 2005, which Yeang designed. A building with two 20-metre-high sky courts that hold trees up to four metres tall, it was tacitly endorsed by the President of Singapore in 2005 when, for the first time, he gave his National Day speech outside his Palace in the uppermost 'pod' of the library. The Library was awarded a GreenMark Platinum Rating (Singapore's equivalent to rating systems such as LEED and BREEAM).

Yeang's current work includes the SOMA Masterplan in Bangalore, India and the DIGI Technical Operations Centre in Kuala Lumpur. He is also currently building the greenest hospital extension in the UK, the Morgan Stanley Clinical Building on Great Ormond Street in London's Bloomsbury, due for completion in 2011. These projects reflect the culmination of ideas developed throughout his earlier works, with a maturation of his ecological aesthetic together with an increased number of green features and a deeper level of biointegration than previously seen. Yeang's current masterplanning work involves the interdependence between buildings and landscapes in new urban districts. An example of this is his design for Premier City in Almaty, the new financial district of Kazakhstan. This 90,000-square-metre site is the first in the country to have ecologically advanced residential towers, and its infrastructure includes a central green belt that links with over 7 million trees throughout the city's streets. This urban park will act as a green 'fissure', enhancing local biodiversity and weaving through the site in a continuous band of vegetation extending up and over buildings.

Many of Yeang's schemes are large projects, but unlike the vast majority of large-scale buildings the world over, all incorporate a judicious balance of vertical landscaping and vegetation as part of his continuous ecoinfrastructure concept. Landscape architects are on the staff of Yeang's practice, but he also works with other landscape architecture firms. Yeang usually designs and configures the vertical and horizontal landscape ecoinfrastructure for all of his projects, as well as designing the landscape layout patterns. Other landscape architects then assist with the selection of species, construction details, irrigation and sustainable drainage systems in the design of bioswales, detention ponds and rainwater harvesting and water management systems.

Yeang has effectively rewritten the rules of engagement between the human built environment and the natural environment. He has opened up a way to perceive each building as 'a three dimensional space with its own analogous metabolism'. He believes that green lungs in cities should not just be open green areas for bringing the natural environment into cities, but rather that they should contribute ecologically. Ideally, green lungs would function as 'enhancements of biodiversity, as greenery for the sequestering of carbon dioxide, and as an integral part of the ecoinfrastructure of the city with ecological corridors and fingers that must be relinked and reconnected to the landscape in the hinterland' using ecobridges and ecoundercrofts. What humans have done, he observes, is to 'fragment the landscape with our streets, roads, buildings and pavements. We need to reverse the process and reconnect nature to make it whole'.

Yeang's approach to architecture has ramifications for the wellbeing and quality of life of users, which are among the most important architectural considerations today. His work is largely geared to specific public buildings used by large numbers of people, such as workspaces and libraries. Through their exposure to Yeang's evolving strategies, clients and users have embraced a closer contact with nature, enhancing their wellbeing. This concept is as old as civilisation, but the current rise in 'biophilia' has enabled design that explores the different ways in which nature can be integrated with buildings. This in turn allows the buildings to be spaces for social and ecological interaction.

Though it is fair to say that one of his critical agendas is to redefine the identity and relationship of architecture with nature, Yeang's buildings are not organic in a traditional way (such as mud huts or adobe dwellings, for example). He is however sympathetic to the idea of organic architecture as part of his pursuit for a new ecological nexus and an ecological aesthetic. He likens the relationship between architecture and nature to that of prosthetic limbs and the human body. This analogy with medical practice places the human built environment in the role of an artificial and synthetic system similar to a prosthesis in medical surgery, where effective biointegration is vital. Yeang explains that the human built environment's equivalent organic host is the biosphere and its ecosystems, with which the human built environment must biointegrate in a seamless and benign way at physical, systematic and temporal levels.

Experts differ in their views about the effectiveness of green technological products, but Yeang argues that these products alone do not solve ecological challenges in a way that is geared to the specific conditions of a given site's ecology and climate. 'Nobody has yet brought the computational systems—the communicational and environmental sensoring software and technologies together with site-specific ecological data and then converted them into form-influencing data', says Yeang. Ecodesign is cross-disciplinary, he explains. It needs someone to guide and crystallise the final result in a way that gives due regard to aesthetics, to the ethos of sustainability and to the social demands of the occupants, making sure these factors are interdependent at a profound level, not just on the surface.

Educational institutions are now moving towards teaching sustainability, but this has been a slow process. 'It is clear that architects came upon this scene late. Most people in practice today are not taught ecology', says Yeang. Bioclimatic design, or designing with climate, was prevalent in the 1950s as an educational topic in architectural schools—but by the late 1960s, before the energy crisis of the 1970s, oil had become so cheap that architects could heat and air-condition their buildings to give comfortable internal conditions without having to consider the climate. Schools of architecture therefore stopped teaching bioclimatic design, and architecture became totally non-responsive to climate. Only in the 1970s were alternative sources of energy pioneered, with new legislation supporting research and development. Long-term scarcity has instilled a questioning of resource exploitation, and slowly architecture is engaging in a debate about energy use that is becoming louder by the day.

Unfortunately, the dominance of engineering and the emphasis on building performance simulations has led to ecologically advanced architecture being perceived as an issue of engineering, rather than as a matter of ecology and other environmental concerns. It is quite common for an engineer to outfit a building with ecogadgetry and call this ecological architecture. This state of play is misleading for young architects.

Accepting climate change has been a slow process for many societies, states *The Anatomy of a Silent Crisis*, a 2009 report by the Global Humanitarian Forum in Geneva. As Kofi Annan, President of the Forum, says in his introduction: 'in industrialised countries, climate change is still considered a solely environmental problem. It is seen as a distant threat that might affect our future. A viewpoint reinforced by pictures of glaciers and polar bears—not human beings'.

Architecture that manifests an ecological awareness, including low energy and zero carbon designs, varies considerably. Yeang's approach is distinct in that he has evolved his own theories, a technical framework that works with his theories, and design interpretations for that technical framework—he thus creates a versatile armature for ecological architecture. These are perhaps his most significant contributions to this field.

Regarding green design as an 'interactions model' requires rigorous environmental monitoring of its inputs, its outputs and their impact on the environment. This is a theoretical model that Yeang has developed and is very committed to. In green design, multi-scalar spatial design skills also come to the fore in order to allow both a greater flexibility and responsiveness in spatial concepts. Concurrently, Yeang's team advances their work through an intensive and constant pursuit of improvement in all aspects of their activities, something learnt from Japanese industry's adherence to *kaizen*, the practice of continuous improvement.

Architects need to understand how to apply integrated thinking concerning buildings and their environmental context as part of a sustainable global ecosystem. The ambitious balance of modernity and nature that forms Yeang's focus in this area requires a new set of ecological criteria. Good work in this field has to go beyond conventional rating systems like LEED or BREEAM criteria, Yeang feels. Accreditation systems may 'contribute to a green built system', but certainly are 'not green architecture in totality'. Yeang's 2007 competition entry for the BIDV Tower in Vietnam, for example, is a cohesive set of strategies for space, function, structure, climate sensitivity, vertical circulation, wind and ventilation, biodiversity, urban ecology and iconicity.

In his public speaking role Yeang regularly encounters concerns from audiences about many things: the cost of green design, its consequences for the city and the landscape, the maintenance of buildings and how vegetation can be effectively integrated. All these concerns can be addressed by a process of cost control. He cautions that 'what could easily become forgotten in the relentless pursuit of the green agenda are the human, societal or the user aspects, which could get neglected or upstaged'.

These are his key priorities in any green design. Yeang personally develops several strands at the same time. The process juggles theory, technical interpretations and the development of ecological aesthetics simultaneously. If one of these strands progresses further than the other, his thoughts are redirected so that other strands can catch up. Similarly his professional commitments are fourfold. He believes that to be a complete architect, 'we need to teach to get new ideas and to expand one's vision in our field of endeavour, to research to enable the development of new ideas, to write to get feedback on our ideas and work, to design and build to physically test our ideas'. Few architects do all of these. 'It is very stressful to do this entire cycle. It demands focus, commitment and sacrifices'. It is precisely this focus, commitment and sacrifice that differentiates Yeang's work from that of others in the field.

Using Yeang as a role model, several young studios are undertaking valuable strategic work in setting clear directions for multidisciplinary socially sustainable design. Further new rules of engagement are being set. The cybernetics of dynamic systems are being reappraised. Simulation studies are being carried out embracing humanitarian causes under a wider brief for emergency architecture. The work of the Spanish practice Ecosistema Arquitectos, Cameron Sinclair's Architects for Humanity, EcoLogic Studio and many others demonstrate this. The commitment to biodiversity and longer time scales by landscape architects such as Field Operations and Gross. Max is stronger than ever. Exploration Architecture's Sahara Forest project shows design thinking extending to desert regions, engaging with geological strategies. William McDonough and Michael Braungart, authors of *Cradle to Cradle*, posit thinking of 'buildings like trees, cities like forests', and in doing so have thrown down the gauntlet (albeit a simplistic one) for commitment to a new paradigm of green architecture. At Futureproofing the City in 2009, Bill Dunster, like many experts in the field, wanted 'to plead with the architectural profession to have a vision and sell it very well'. He believes in survivalist architecture that invests in ecological services so that buildings can continue without fossil fuel, radically restructuring a global industry with off-grid solutions and affordable components shared between countries.

To put this in an historical context, Yeang points out that 'today architects can at least find firms of M&E engineers conversant with ecotechnologies and engineering to help them make their designs at a minimal level internationally accredited as green'. In 1975 when he was starting out in business, many of the ecotechnologies available today simply did not exist. Solar photovoltaic cells were in their experimental infancy and were too expensive to be viable. Wind generators had numerous teething problems in implementation. Green materials—those that are environmentally benign in their production with high recycled content—were not yet readily available. Neither was 'the idea of embodied energy in materials and the ecology of incorporating landscape into buildings fully understood'.

Consequently Yeang and his team had to invent or make do with what was available, using friends who were researchers at universities to test their environmental performances and to do CFD (Computational Fluid Dynamics) simulations for them. Today most engineering firms have the necessary software to carry these out in-house. Apart from the lack of good engineering support in the 1970s and 1980s, Yeang had to overcome the difficulties in getting affordable ecoengineering systems and green materials, as there were few available on the market. His ideas provoked incredulity from clients at first, as there had been little theoretical or research work done. His peers tended to regard Yeang and his team as mavericks pursuing goals they did not understand.

Over more than a third of a century, Yeang has paid consistent attention in his work to evolving ecological architecture and urban design. His books, among them *Ecodesign: A Manual for Ecological Design*, outline the fundamental premises for ecodesign, and argue the rationale for a deep green design to be considered at the outset. Now that we are obliged to retrofit and futureproof our world, the impact of Yeang's integrated roles—as architect, researcher, author and green spokesperson—can be fully seen. He is a pioneering, visionary contributor to the enrichment of the holistic ecological and spatial possibilities of our cities and built environment. Yeang's extensive work is testimony to his success in convincing the development community of the imperative to expand the ecological horizons of society, and of his own unerring commitment to do green design differently for a very good reason.

Typology of Plans

Spire Edge—India

BIDV Tower—Vietnam

Solaris—Singapore

GyeongGi Provincial
Government Office—Korea

L Tower—Malaysia

Damansara Garden
Residences—Malaysia

Eco Bay Complex—United
Arab Emirates

KIA Tower—Kuwait

Plaza of Nations—Canada

P Tower—Malaysia

Shenzhen Garden City—China

DB Tower—Malaysia

G Tower—China

Buildings and Projects

Spire Edge

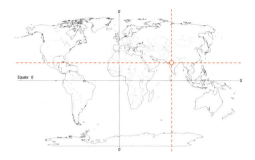

Location
Manesar, Gurgaon, India

Climate Zone
Subtropical

Vegetation Zone
Subtropical Forest

No. of Storeys
23

Areas
GFA   : 22,559 m²
NFA   : 17,165 m²

Site Area
4765 m²

Plot Ratio
1:4.7

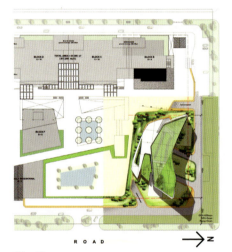

Site Plan

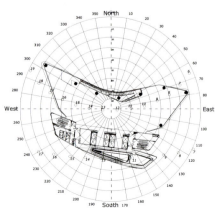

Sun Path

The Spire Edge office tower stands as an iconic landmark for a new IT park located in Manesar, Gurgaon, India. Scheduled for completion in 2011, the tower is comprised of 23 storeys accommodating offices, an auditorium, galleries and other facilities. Key design features include a zone of continuous greenery that ascends from the heart of the surrounding IT park complex up to the building's highest roof gardens. These interconnected landscaped ramps provide the project with ecological diversity, outdoor terraces and interactive gardens, thereby enhancing the project's creative environment.

Continuous Green Ramps

The south façade of the building features continuous landscaped ramps that bring pedestrians and vegetation from the basement up to a lush roof garden. On the tower's north side, greenery links to the roof garden via a series of green systems that include vegetated green walls, landscaped ramps, pedestrian ramps and a series of landscaped sky terraces. These systems act as thermal buffers, protecting the building envelope from direct solar heat gain, and create event spaces and areas for relaxation.

Ecocells

There are two ecocells located at the north and south of the building where the spiral ramps meet the ground. These vegetated ramps extend into the basement levels. Ecocells allow vegetation, daylight and natural ventilation to extend into the car-park levels below. The lowest level of the ecocells contains storage tanks and pump rooms that support the project's rainwater recycling system.

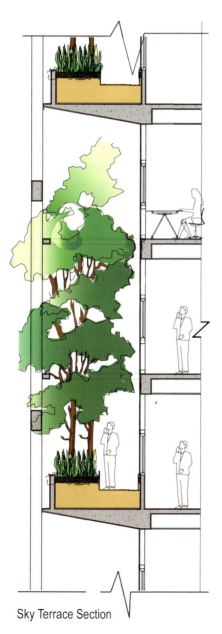

Sky Terrace Section

S
P
I
R
E

E
D
G
E

North View

Site Plan

Level 1

Level 2

Level 3

Level 4

Level 5

Level 6

Level 7

Level 8

Level 9

Level 10

Level 11

Level 12

Level 13

Level 14

Level 15

Level 16

Level 17

Level 18

Level 19

Roof Garden

Pod Level

Roof Canopy

S
P
I
R
E

E
D
G
E

N

Summary of Plans

Roof Gardens

The building's extensive gardens allow for interaction between its occupants and nature, offering opportunities to experience the tower's external environments and to enjoy views of the adjacent IT park. The roof gardens and sky courts are further subdivided into creative meeting spaces and multi-use terraces. A series of sky courts in the north façade also provide a variety of outdoor environments for office users' creative and social interactions.

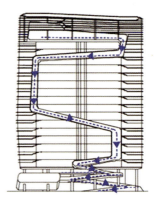

Rainwater Harvesting

The tower is designed to be as self sufficient as possible in terms of water use. It achieves this via an integrated system of rainwater harvesting and reuse. The project's green ramps and landscaped terraces act as filtration and collection devices, channelling rainwater into tanks located in the basement. This harvested rainwater will then be used to irrigate the building's extensive landscaped areas, significantly reducing the project's consumption of potable water.

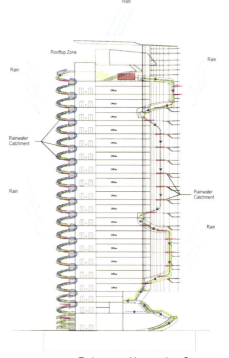

Rainwater Harvesting System

East View

Landscape Features

1. Vegetated Rooftop
2. Vegetated Green Ramp
3. Ascending Green Belt

Water Infrastructure

1. Rooftop Zone Water Collector
2. Rainwater Storage Tank
3. Rainwater Catchment Scallop
4. Filtered Water Storage Tank

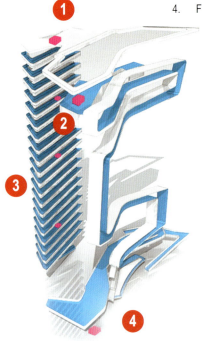

Sunshades

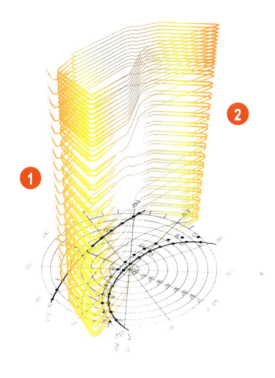

Superstructure

1. Cores

S
P
I
R
E

E
D
G
E

North Elevation

South Elevation

BIDV Tower

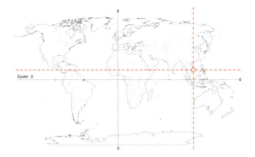

Location
Ho Chi Minh City, Vietnam

Climate Zone
Tropical

Vegetation Zone
Rainforest

No. of Storeys
40

Areas
GFA   : 35,311 m²
NFA   : 27,380 m²

Site Area
2686 m²

Plot Ratio
1:3

Site Plan

Sun Path

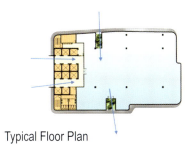

Typical Floor Plan

The 40 storey BIDV Tower is composed of three different functions with integrated social spaces and landscaped areas. The ground floor to Level 4 are occupied by the Bank for Investment and Development of Vietnam (BIDV). Levels 5 and 6 contain international conference halls and seminar rooms. The remaining floors house leased office spaces and are topped by a roof garden with recreational areas and dining rooms. The tower is located on Nguyen Hue Boulevard, an important artery of Ho Chi Minh City. The primary design concept involved the social and physical integration of the boulevard into the building. Rising with the tower, the boulevard infuses each floor with greenery before descending to merge back into the city streets.

Wind Funnels

The project's ecological features include wind funnels, ecocells, sunshade louvres, sky courts and roof gardens. Wind funnels, vertical indentations in the building's perimeter, help ensure that all common areas, including lift lobbies, toilets and fire stairs, are naturally ventilated. They also help channel wind across upper floor plates to effectively cross-ventilate office workspaces. Wing walls in the back and sides of the tower further assist in channeling wind directly into the building. Ecocells are a passive method of bringing sunlight and fresh air into the basement levels of the building. Sky courts allow building occupants to enjoy greenery, and contribute to an efficient strategy for passive cooling along the building's façade. Greenery-filled gardens flanking the wing walls cool air as it is channelled into the building. Operable windows control the amount of fresh air passing into the workspaces. Should there be a power failure, these passive strategies ensure that the tower will still function comfortably. Together, these features represent a proven strategy for significantly reducing operating costs and providing a comfortable environment for the building's occupants.

B
I
D
V

T
O
W
E
R

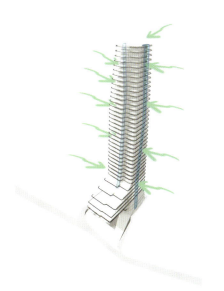

Naturally Ventilated Cores

Northwest View

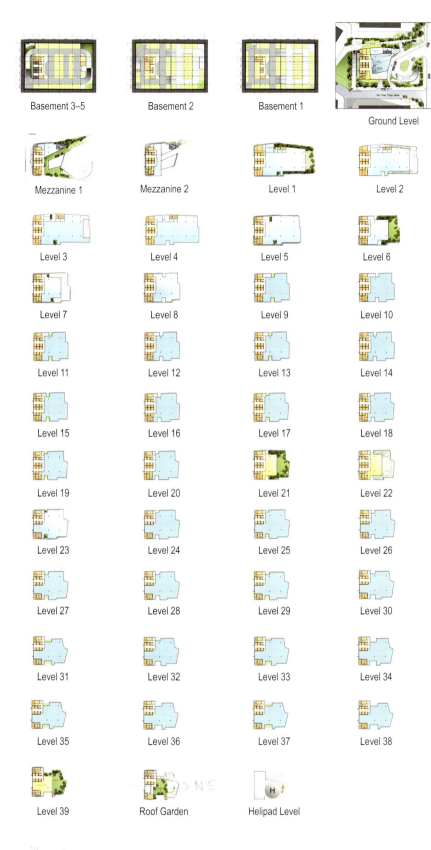

Basement 3–5

Basement 2

Basement 1

Ground Level

Mezzanine 1

Mezzanine 2

Level 1

Level 2

Level 3

Level 4

Level 5

Level 6

Level 7

Level 8

Level 9

Level 10

Level 11

Level 12

Level 13

Level 14

Level 15

Level 16

Level 17

Level 18

Level 19

Level 20

Level 21

Level 22

Level 23

Level 24

Level 25

Level 26

Level 27

Level 28

Level 29

Level 30

Level 31

Level 32

Level 33

Level 34

Level 35

Level 36

Level 37

Level 38

Level 39

Roof Garden

Helipad Level

B
I
D
V

T
O
W
E
R

Summary of Plans

Sun Shading Concept

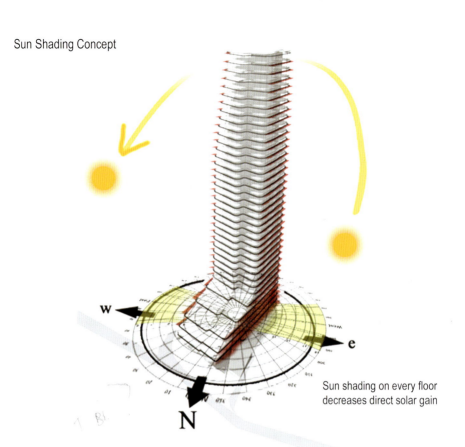

Sun shading on every floor
decreases direct solar gain

Ecological Concept

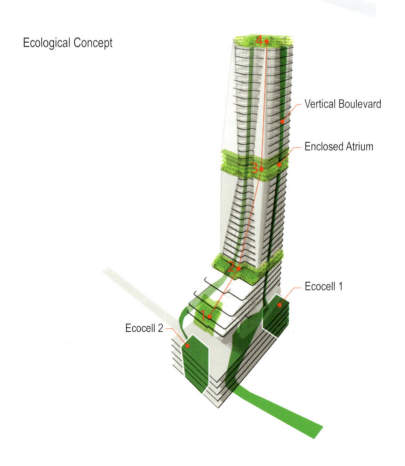

Vertical Boulevard

Enclosed Atrium

Ecocell 1

Ecocell 2

Level 21 (Sky Lobby)

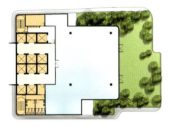

Level 6

Podium Level 1

The Vertical Boulevard

Continuous zones of vegetation connect plants from the boulevard to the roof of the tower. This vertical landscaping rises along the wing walls of the 'vertical boulevard' that spans the entire height of BIDV Tower. This integrated greenery further enhances the cooling effect of the sky terraces, lowering the temperature of wind passing through them into adjacent workspaces.

A series of sky courts are designed to flow down the sides of the tower. With recessed balconies and full-height glazed doors opening out from adjacent offices, they act as 'parks in the sky' and serve as interstitial zones between inside and outside areas. Sky courts provide occupiable areas for relaxation as well as views of greenery and plants from internal workstations. Planting within the east and west façades reduces heat gain from exposure to direct sunlight and helps prevent glare from negatively impacting on workspace productivity.

The benefits of sky courts are:
- shading for the building
- emergency evacuation zones
- areas for planting and landscaping
- flexible interstitial zones for future expansion
- to provide direct experiences of the external environment on upper floors and views to outside gardens

B
I
D
V

T
O
W
E
R

Entrance View

Night View

Ecological Features

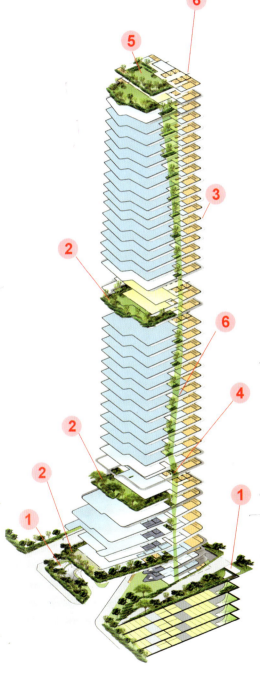

1. Ecocells

- Allow daylighting and natural ventilation to penetrate into the building
- Link vegetation on the roof garden to internal spaces of the building
- A rainwater harvesting tank stores rainwater for reuse and recycling

2. Sky Courts

- Allow interaction between nature and building occupants
- Provide opportunities to experience the external environment and enjoy views

3. Sun Shading

- Reduces heat gain from direct sunlight, and hence the energy needed to cool the building
- Reduces glare

4. The Vertical Boulevard

- Planted terraces carry soil and vegetation from existing ground-level greenery to upper levels of the building
- Reduces ambient air temperatures during summer
- Reduces heat loss during winter
- Creates healthy exterior microclimates for the building's occupants

5. Roof Garden

- Vegetation on the roof helps reduce heat gain from conduction while providing a relaxing area for the community to enjoy

6. Wind Funnels

- Protruding walls channel wind into building core and service areas
- Provide cross ventilation for offices
- A sustainable natural ventilation strategy with low maintenance costs

B
I
D
V

T
O
W
E
R

Ecocells

Ecocells are vertical cellular voids or slots integrated into the building's podium, located between the ground floor and the roof garden (over the podium). These voids, for example on the bottom right and top left of the building, allow natural daylight to penetrate the full depth of the basement levels. In doing so, the ecocells serve as excellent devices for the ventilation of lower levels where stale, warm air rises and is replaced with fresh outside air. This sustainable, passive ventilation strategy requires no additional cost.

In addition to enhancing natural ventilation, ecocells allow greenery to extend into the upper basement levels. Planted landscapes on the ground floor weave their way in and out of the basement levels to create seamless physical green connections. These shrubs, bushes and grasses introduce biological air filters into otherwise dingy subterranean spaces.

Natural Daylighting

To bring natural daylight into the inner depths of the floor

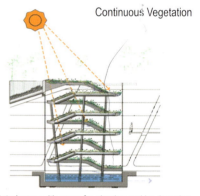

Continuous Vegetation

Vegetated ramp with areas for planting and landscaping to experience external environment directly

Natural Ventilation

Natural ventilation of carpark and exhibition spaces

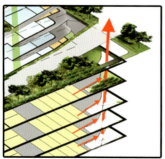

Carpark Ventilation Diagram

Street Level View

Northwest Elevation

Ground Floor ▼   0.0m

Southeast Elevation

Mezzanine Level

Banking Hall

Solaris

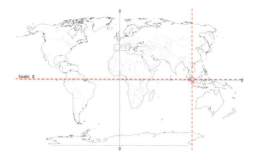

Location
one-north, Singapore

Climate Zone
Tropical

Vegetation Zone
Rainforest

No. of Storeys
15

Areas
GFA   : 51,282 m²
NFA   : 42,564 m²

Site Area
7734 m²

Plot Ratio
1:7

Site Plan

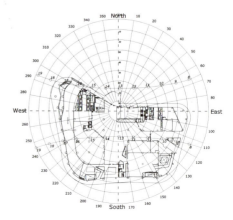

Sun Path

Central Atrium

Solaris is comprised of two tower blocks separated by a grand, naturally ventilated central atrium. Office floors are linked by a series of sky bridges that span the atrium at upper floors. The building's overall energy consumption will represent a reduction of over 33% compared to local precedents, and the project has been awarded the Singapore Building Control Authority's GreenMark Platinum rating. With over 8000 square metres of landscaping, Solaris introduces vegetated areas that exceed the size of the project's site.

The project stands as a dramatic demonstration of the possibilities inherent in an ecological approach to building design. Solaris will become a vibrant focal point for the one-north community through the introduction of open interactive spaces, the creative use of skylights and courtyards for natural light and ventilation and a continuous spiral landscaped ramp. The ramp is an extension of one-north Park across the street. Together they form an ecological nexus that joins with an escalating sequence of roof gardens and sky terraces that interpenetrate the building's façade. With its extensive ecoinfrastructure, sustainable design features and innovative vertical green concept, Solaris strives to enhance its site's existing ecosystems, rather than replace them.

SOLARIS

Pocket Park / Plaza

Ground level landscaping, linking to one-north Park across the street, allows for cross ventilation of the ground-floor plaza and provides a venue for social and interactive events.

Extensive Sun-Shading Louvres

The project's climate-responsive façade design originated with analysis of the site's sun-path. Singapore is on the equator and the sun-path is almost exactly east–west. Façade studies analysing the solar path determined the shape and depth of the sunshade louvres, which also double as light-shelves. This solar shading strategy further reduces heat transfer across the building's low-e double-glazed perimeter façade, contributing to a low External Thermal Transfer Value (ETTV) of 39 watts/m^2. In conjunction with the spiral landscaped ramp, sky gardens and deep overhangs, the sunshade louvres also assist in establishing comfortable microclimates in habitable spaces along the building's exterior. The combined length of the building's sun-shade louvres exceeds 10 kilometers.

Roof Gardens and Corner Sky Terraces

Vertical landscaping acts as a thermal buffer and creates event spaces and areas for relaxation. These extensive gardens allow for interaction between the building's occupants and nature, offering the occupants opportunities to experience the external environment and enjoy views of the treetops of one-north Park. As it reaches each corner of the building the spiral ramp expands into generous double-volume sky terraces. Upon completion, the sum of the project's vegetated areas will exceed the footprint of the site on which the building sits.

Rainwater Harvesting / Recycling

The building's extensive landscaped areas are irrigated via a large-scale rainwater recycling system. Rainwater is collected from the drainage downpipes of the perimeter landscaped ramp and from the roof of tower B via siphonic drainage. It is stored in rooftop tanks and in the lowest basement level, beneath the ecocell. A storage capacity of more than 700 cubic meters allows for more than five days of irrigation via recycled water

Aerial View

View from one-north Park

Ground Level

Basement 2

Basement 1

Basement Mezzanine

Level 2

Level 3

Level 4

Level 5

Level 6

Level 7

Level 8

Level 9

Level 10

Level 11

Level 12

Level 13

Level 14

Level 15

Level 16

Roof Level

Summary of Plans

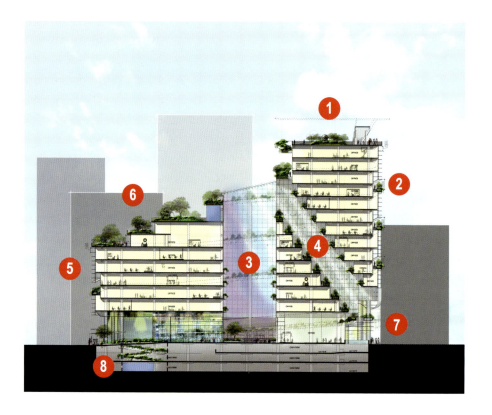

1. Roof Garden
2. Continuous Vertical Landscaping (1.5 Kilometre Urban Ecosystem)
3. Naturally-Ventilated Day-Lit Atrium
4. Solar Shaft
5. Climate-Responsive Façade
6. Sky Terraces
7. Verandahway (Semi-Enclosed Tropical Walkway)
8. Ecocell and Rainwater Harvesting

Green Ramp View

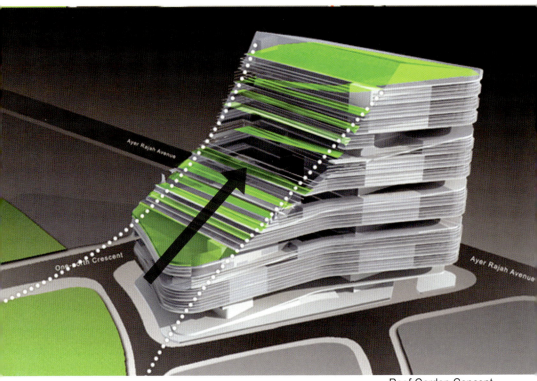

Roof Garden Concept

Continuous Green Ramp Concept

Corner Sky Terrace Section

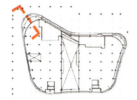

Green Ramp Section

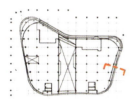

Ayer Rajah Avenue View

GyeongGi Provincial Government Office

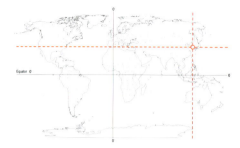

Location
GyeongGi, South Korea

Climate Zone
Temperate

Vegetation Zone
Evergreen trees

No. of Storeys
46

Areas
GFA   : 102,416 m²
NFA   : 81,200 m²

Site Area
136,805 m²

Site Plan

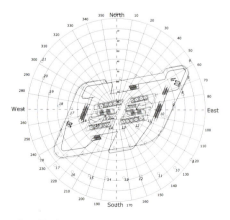

Sun Path

Night View

This design uniquely integrates nature with human life, binding them together with sustainable ecoengineering and creating a pleasurable lifestyle and high quality environment for people using the spaces and facilities. The design also provides spaces for culture, enabling a multitude of cultural activities to take place here throughout the year. At the same time, it provides appropriate climate-responsive enclosures that give the building its own unique cultural identity.

As the effects of climate change and urban heat islands continue to escalate, the urban forests in this design will carry out essential roles in cooling, shading, pollution sequestration and drought and flood protection. Ecologically, the design repairs and reconnects existing site vegetation and forests as living systems within a new ecological nexus. It strives to create new habitats with biodiversity targets to provide landscapes blended within a new ecologically responsive built environment. This use of biodiversity targets and the creation of a series of habitats, based on an analysis of local species and site ecology, is an approach to ecological design that has been developed specifically for this project.

GYEONGGI

Aerial View

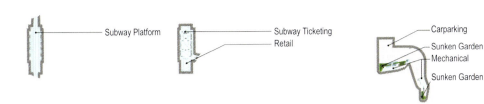

Basement 4   Basement 3   Basement 2

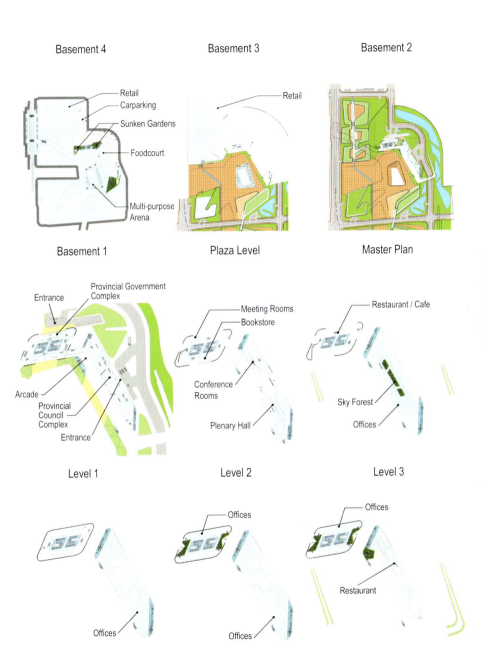

Basement 1   Plaza Level   Master Plan

Level 1   Level 2   Level 3

Level 4   Level 5   Level 6

Summary of Plans

Sky Forest View

Level 7

Level 8

Level 9 Level 10 Level 11 Level 12 Level 13 Level 14

Level 15 Level 16 Level 17 Level 18 Level 19 Level 20

Level 21 Level 22 Level 23 Level 24 Level 25 Level 26

Level 27 Level 28 Level 29 Level 30 Level 31 Level 32

Level 33 Level 34 Level 35 Level 36 Level 37 Level 38

Level 39 Level 40 Level 41 Level 42 Level 43 Level 44

Level 45 Level 46

Summary of Plans

A holistic green design is created by weaving four infrastructures into a whole.

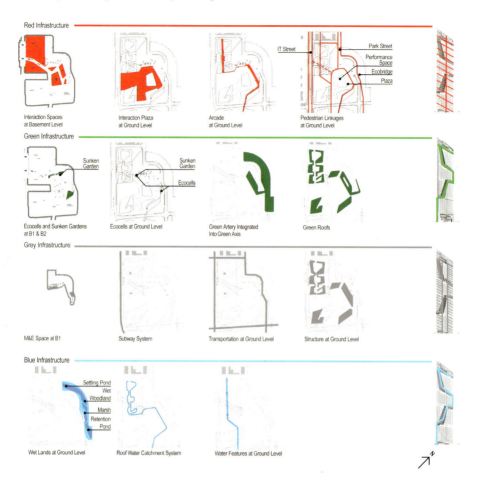

Red Infrastructure

Interaction Spaces at Basement Level
Interaction Plaza at Ground Level
Arcade at Ground Level
Pedestrian Linkages at Ground Level

IT Street
Park Street
Performance Space
Ecobridge
Plaza

Green Infrastructure

Ecocells and Sunken Gardens at B1 & B2
Ecocells at Ground Level
Green Artery Integrated Into Green Axis
Green Roofs

Sunken Garden
Sunken Garden
Ecocells

Grey Infrastructure

M&E Space at B1
Subway System
Transportation at Ground Level
Structure at Ground Level

Blue Infrastructure

Wet Lands at Ground Level
Roof Water Catchment System
Water Features at Ground Level

Settling Pond
Wet Woodland
Marsh
Retention Pond

Red Infrastructure

The human infrastructure provides a pleasurable experience for users by incorporating a variety of facilities, such as continuous covered pedestrian arcades, cycle routes and large open public plazas. These create seamless spatial transitions between recreational, leisure and performance spaces within major public zones.

Grey Infrastructure

The ecoengineering infrastructure mitigates the building's overall energy consumption via an active system of naturally ventilated cores and common areas. Further to this, the transportation systems on site consist of light rail, buses, covered walkways and roads.

Green Infrastructure

This is a state-of-the-art green design (ecoinfrastructure) that originates from the surrounding ecological biome and extends into the site with ecobridges and undercrofts. In doing so, the extension of existing habitats creates a High Tech Green Urban Artery, providing an uninterrupted flow of vegetation and species within and around the site. The use of ecocells, sunken gardens, sky forests and parks allows daylight to reach into deep interstitial spaces, providing healthier atmospheres for staff and visitors.

Blue Infrastructure

Integrated into the green infrastructure, the water infrastructure functions to harvest rainwater, potable and non-potable water from all buildings on site. Subsequent to the harvesting process, the water is treated and redistributed for irrigation and other non-potable uses.

Ground Level View

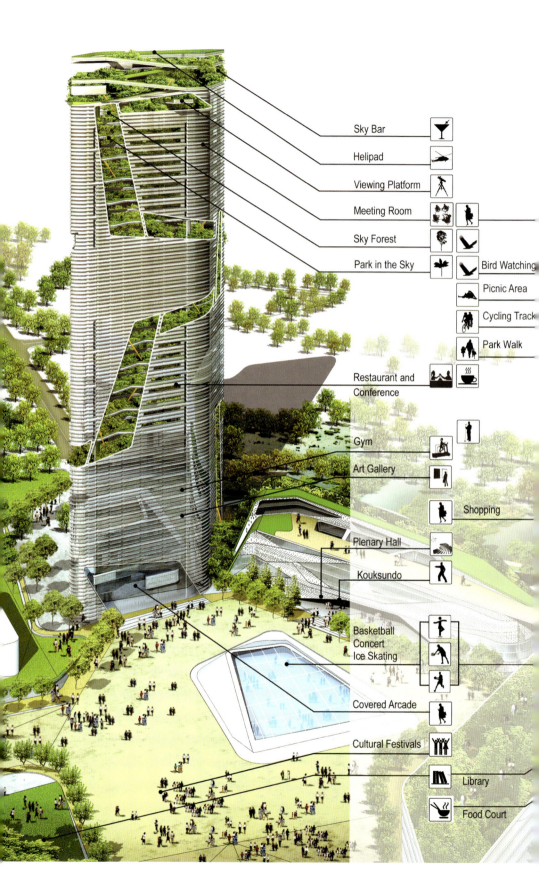

Sky Bar

Helipad

Viewing Platform

Meeting Room

Sky Forest

Park in the Sky

Bird Watching

Picnic Area

Cycling Track

Park Walk

Restaurant and
Conference

Gym

Art Gallery

Shopping

Plenary Hall

Kouksundo

Basketball
Concert
Ice Skating

Covered Arcade

Cultural Festivals

Library

Food Court

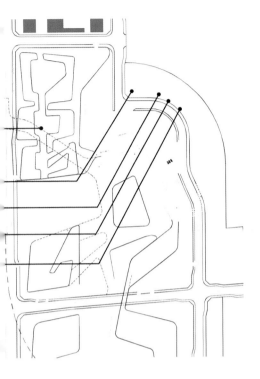

Pleasure Zones

Clearly defined zones have been designed to provide pleasurable experiences for the community. The continuation of the adjacent green corridor forms a green belt that links wet woodlands, settling ponds, the Provincial Council and the Provincial Government buildings into a series of recreational, commercial and cultural spaces that make up the pleasure zones. Activities that can be undertaken in these zones include bird watching, having a picnic near water features in the wet woodlands, watching cultural performances, shopping, dining, ice skating, enjoying a quiet afternoon of reading in the world-class library, yoga or enjoying a show at the water theatre. All of these activities provide people with pleasurable experiences that integrate culture with high-tech, deep green ecoinfrastructure.

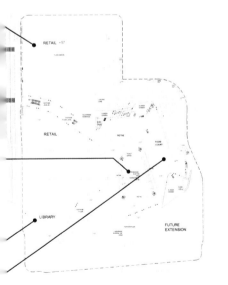

Icon Key

 Shopping

 Library

 Restaurant

 Dance Performance

 Badminton Court

 Basketball Court

 Gym

 Art Gallery

 Meditation

 Plenary Hall

 Kouksundo Room

 Park in the Sky

Sky Terrace

Meeting

 Park Walk

 Conference

 Performance Plaza

 Cafe

 Lecture Hall

 Bird Watching Park

 Yoga Hall

 Cycling Track

 Helipad

 Bar and Lounge

Viewing Platform

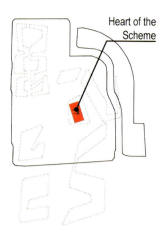

1. Multipurpose Arena
as Heart of the Scheme

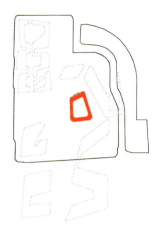

2. Tiered Seating
for Multipurpose Arena

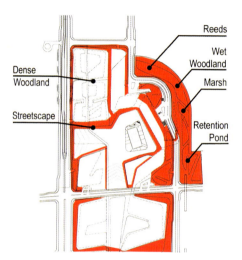

Reeds

Wet Woodland

Dense Woodland

Marsh

Streetscape

Retention Pond

5. Landscape and Habitats

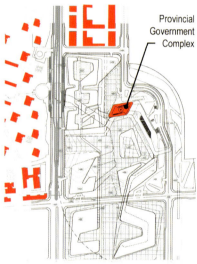

Provincial Government Complex

6. Provincial Government Complex

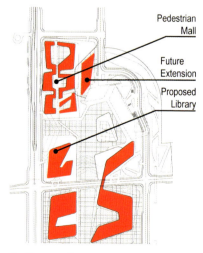

Pedestrian Mall

Future Extension

Proposed Library

9. Surrounding Buildings and Figure Ground Relationship

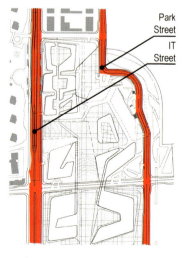

Park Street

IT Street

10. IT Street and Park Street

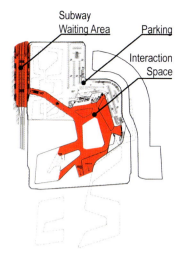

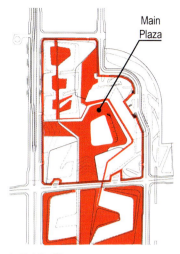

3. Concourse Level
From Train and Bus Station to Underground Plaza

4. Public Plaza

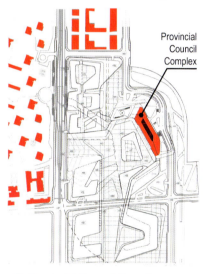

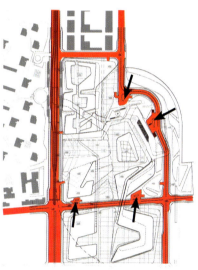

7. Provincial Council Complex

8. Ground Level Roads and Dropoffs

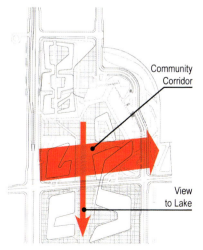

11. Views

12. Arcade

Biodiversity Targets

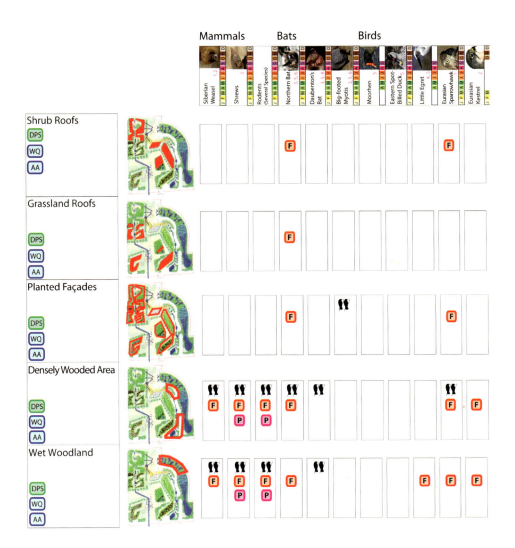

Mammals — Siberian Weasel, Shrews, Rodents (Several Species)
Bats — Northern Bat, Daubenton's Bat, Big-footed Myotis
Birds — Moorhen, Eastern Spot-Billed Duck, Little Egret, Eurasian Sparrowhawk, Eurasian Kestrel

Shrub Roofs — DPS, WQ, AA
Grassland Roofs — DPS, WQ, AA
Planted Façades — DPS, WQ, AA
Densely Wooded Area — DPS, WQ, AA
Wet Woodland — DPS, WQ, AA

Codes

1 Top of the food chain for small Mammals
2 Top of the food chain for small Birds
3 Top of the food chain for Invertebrates
4 Top of the food chain for Fish/Amphibians
5 Use of artifical refuges
6 Dependent on good water quality
7 Rarity
8 Dependent on specific food plants
9 Song

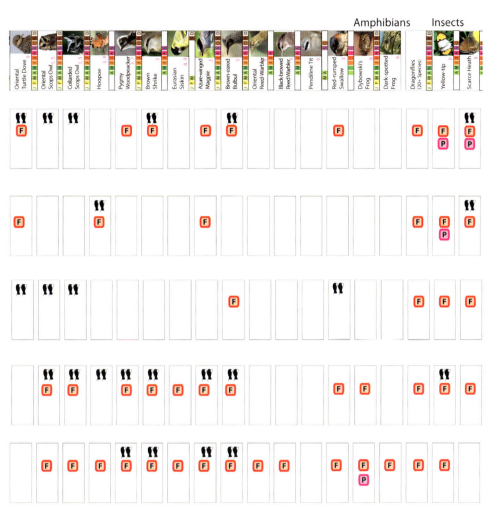

Amphibians   Insects

| Oriental Turtle Dove | Oriental Scops Owl | Collared Scops Owl | Hoopoe | Pygmy Woodpecker | Brown Shrike | Eurasian Siskin | Azure-winged Magpie | Brown-eared Bulbul | Oriental Reed-Warbler | Black-browed Reed-Warbler | Penduline Tit | Red-rumped Swallow | Dybowski's Frog | Dark-spotted Frog | Dragonflies (20+ Species) | Yellow-tip | Scarce Heath |

G
Y
E
O
N
G
G
I

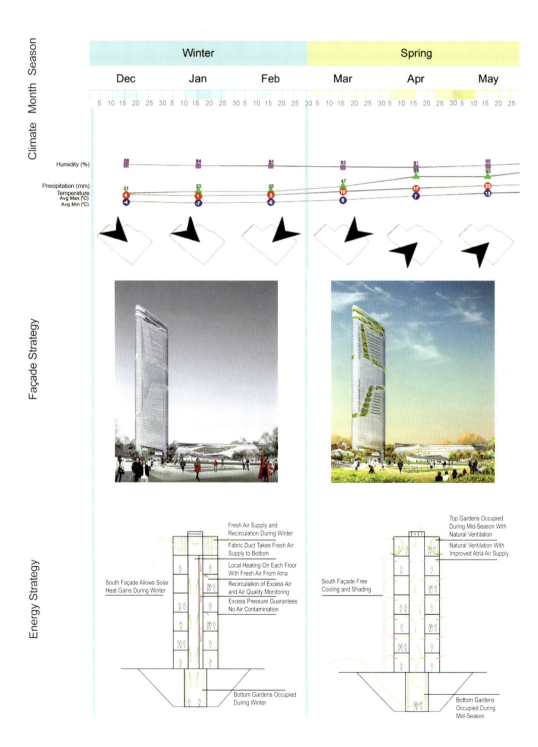

Climate | Month | Season

	Winter			Spring		
	Dec	Jan	Feb	Mar	Apr	May

Humidity (%)
Precipitation (mm)
Temperature
Avg Max (°C)
Avg Min (°C)

Façade Strategy

Energy Strategy

Fresh Air Supply and Recirculation During Winter

Fabric Duct Takes Fresh Air Supply to Bottom

Local Heating On Each Floor With Fresh Air From Atria

South Façade Allows Solar Heat Gains During Winter

Recirculation of Excess Air and Air Quality Monitoring

Excess Pressure Guarantees No Air Contamination

Bottom Gardens Occupied During Winter

Top Gardens Occupied During Mid-Season With Natural Ventilation

Natural Ventilation With Improved Atria Air Supply

South Façade Free Cooling and Shading

Bottom Gardens Occupied During Mid-Season

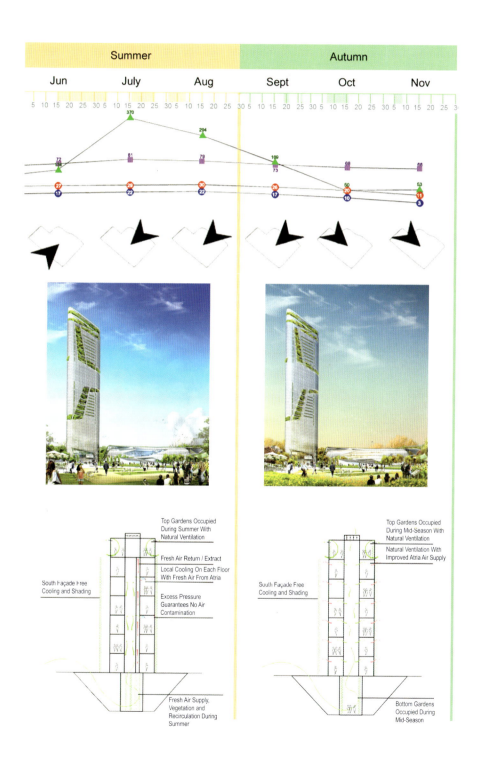

Summer			Autumn		
Jun	July	Aug	Sept	Oct	Nov

Top Gardens Occupied During Summer With Natural Ventilation

Fresh Air Return / Extract

Local Cooling On Each Floor With Fresh Air From Atria

Excess Pressure Guarantees No Air Contamination

South Façade Free Cooling and Shading

Fresh Air Supply, Vegetation and Recirculation During Summer

Top Gardens Occupied During Mid-Season With Natural Ventilation

Natural Ventilation With Improved Atria Air Supply

South Façade Free Cooling and Shading

Bottom Gardens Occupied During Mid-Season

G
Y
E
O
N
G
G
I

GyeongGi Provincial Government Offices

Entrance View

L Tower

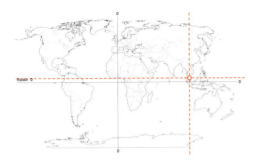

Location
Kuala Lumpur, Malaysia

Climate Zone
Tropical

Vegetation Zone
Rainforest

No. of Storeys
45 (Tower 1) and 42 (Tower 2)

Areas
GFA   : 146,750 m²
NFA   : 117,400 m²

Site Area
18,342 m²

Plot Ratio
1:8

Site Plan

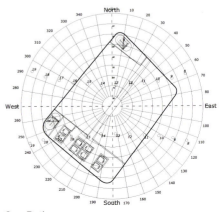

Sun Path

The aim of this development is to create a world-class mixed-use space containing offices, a hotel, serviced apartments, retail and a multi-purpose hall within an interactive green park.

The green footprint is maximised by a green park that weaves through the towers, crowning the apex with roof gardens that create a three dimensional integrated park. This park serves not only the proposed development but also the surrounding community. It will encourage a creative social environment, improving the lifestyle quality of the entire neighbourhood.

Integrated green terraces serve as relaxing and innovative environments for the end users. They are positioned strategically in both the hotel and office towers, and are linked to the lower parks.

The two iconic towers are remarkable physical landmarks for this location and will serve as a focal point for future development.

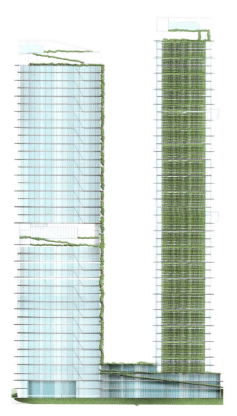

West Elevation

L
T
O
W
E
R

Front View

Master Plan

Basement 5

Basement 2 - 4

Basement 1

Level 1

Level 2

Level 3

Level 4

Level 5

L
T
O
W
E
R

Summary of Plans

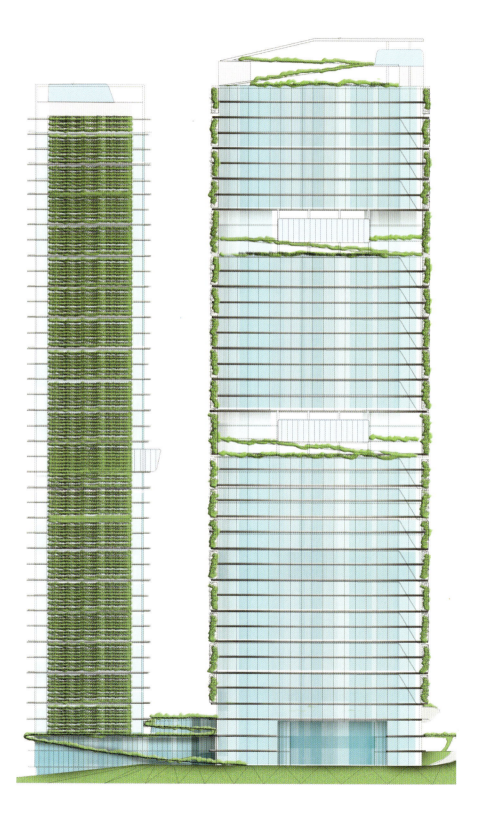

West Elevation

Levels 6-21

Level 22

Level 23

Level 24

Levels 25-34 and 38-45

Level 35

Level 36

Level 37

Roof Plan

Roof Garden

Roof Canopy and Helipad

Levels 6-19

Level 20

Level 21

Level 22

Roof Plan

Roof Garden

Roof Canopy and Helipad

L
T
O
W
E
R

N

Summary of Plans

Plaza View

Damansara Garden Residences

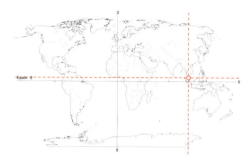

Location
Kuala Lumpur, Malaysia

Climate Zone
Tropical

Vegetation Zone
Rainforest

No. of Storeys
22

Areas
GFA   : 138,036 m²
NFA   : 117,331 m²

Site Area
35,394 m²

Plot Ratio
1:3.9

Site Plan

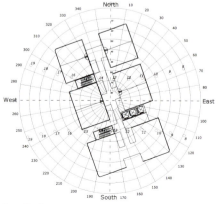

Sun Path

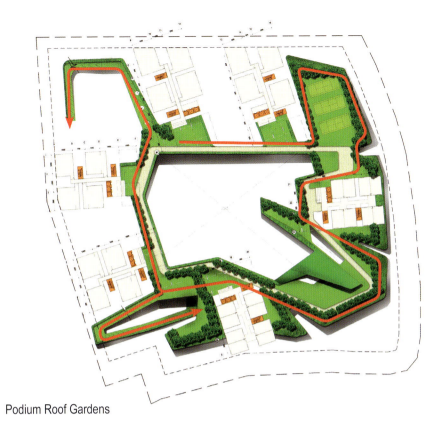

Podium Roof Gardens

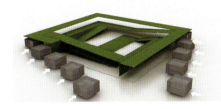

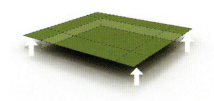

Massing Diagrams

The Damansara Garden Residences are a multi-generational integrated development with six residential tower blocks that rise from a podium containing lifestyle facilities, restaurants and retail shops. The design concept is based on an elevated and folded ground plane that establishes continuous ecological bands throughout the site. These landscaped areas are interwoven with the podium's facilities and leisure gardens, providing amenities for the residences above. Dynamic variations in the levels of the folded landscape create unique spaces and buffers for the activity zones within the development that target specific groups of residents. Examples of these include childcare facilties for families, relaxation and social spaces for the elderly and nightlife areas for young adults. Vegetated walls that are 60 metres high extend the greenery upwards from the podium roof to connect with gardens atop each of the towers.

Aerial View

Designing a Lifestyle for Three Generations

Creating a Unique Lifestyle for Single People Purchasers and Dwellers: A Day in the Life of a Single Person

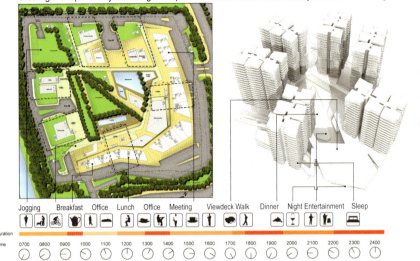

Jogging	Breakfast	Office	Lunch	Office	Meeting	Viewdeck Walk	Dinner	Night Entertainment	Sleep

Duration

Time: 0700 0800 0900 1000 1100 1200 1300 1400 1500 1600 1700 1800 1900 2000 2100 2200 2300 2400

Creating a Unique Lifestyle for Family Purchasers and Dwellers: A Day in the Life of a Family

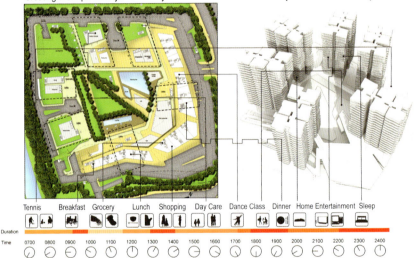

Tennis	Breakfast	Grocery	Lunch	Shopping	Day Care	Dance Class	Dinner	Home Entertainment	Sleep

Duration

Time: 0700 0800 0900 1000 1100 1200 1300 1400 1500 1600 1700 1800 1900 2000 2100 2200 2300 2400

Creating a Unique Lifestyle for Elderly Purchasers and Dwellers: A Day in the Life of an Elderly Person

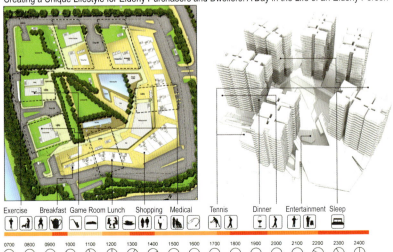

Exercise	Breakfast	Game Room	Lunch	Shopping	Medical	Tennis	Dinner	Entertainment	Sleep

Duration

Time: 0700 0800 0900 1000 1100 1200 1300 1400 1500 1600 1700 1800 1900 2000 2100 2200 2300 2400

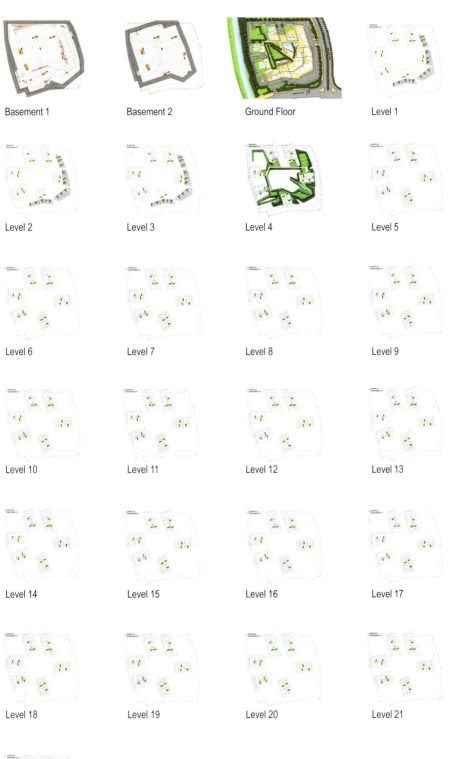

Basement 1

Basement 2

Ground Floor

Level 1

Level 2

Level 3

Level 4

Level 5

Level 6

Level 7

Level 8

Level 9

Level 10

Level 11

Level 12

Level 13

Level 14

Level 15

Level 16

Level 17

Level 18

Level 19

Level 20

Level 21

Roof

DAMANSARA GARDEN RESIDENCES

Summary of Plans

Plaza View

Interior View

Eco Bay Complex

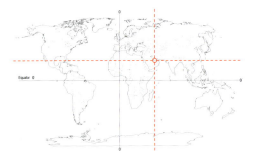

Location
Abu Dhabi, United Arab Emirates

Climate Zone
Desert

Vegetation Zone
Semi Desert-Shrub

No. of Storeys
42

Areas
GFA   : 227,000 m^2
NFA   : 154,000 m^2

Site Area
45,300 m^2

Plot Ratio
1:5

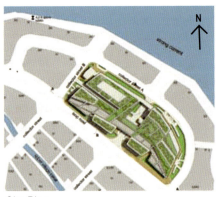

Site Plan

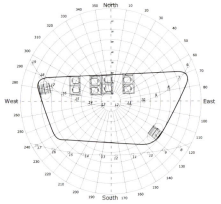

Sun Path

This project consists of five towers: two office towers, two residential towers and one hotel tower on a six-storey podium. The design concept is based on the idea of a 'green oasis of ecological living'. This oasis is conceived as a network of passively cooled, enclosed vertical atrium gardens and public spaces beginning with a large plaza at ground level. The gardens then wind their way up to the sky as a series of pocket parks, floating within each of the five towers, to a rooftop garden and also downwards to the basements. Given the basic premise that for many months of the year Abu Dhabi is too hot for prolonged outdoor activity, the proposed environment is adaptable to the full range of local climatic conditions.

Whereas most mixed-use developments are based on one of two standard typologies—either storefronts accessed directly from the street or enclosed climate-controlled shopping malls—Eco Bay represents a third option suitable for the climatic and urban conditions of Abu Dhabi. The project consists of variably enclosed and passively cooled pedestrian streets and courtyard atriums, around which the various programs and buildings are organised. The project's objectives were firstly to create lifecycle energy savings, and secondly to create a strong visual symbol of a healthy and holistic lifestyle. This symbol then becomes the overiding identity of Eco Bay. The resulting bioclimatic design focuses on low-energy systems of passive cooling and also on the literal 'greening' of the site in the form of its vertical gardens.

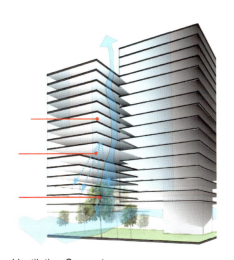

Ventilation Concept

Ground Floor

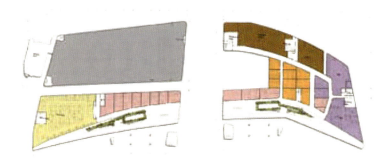

Level 1

Level 2

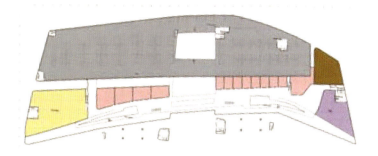

Level 3

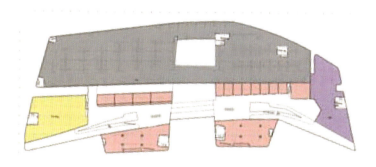

Level 4

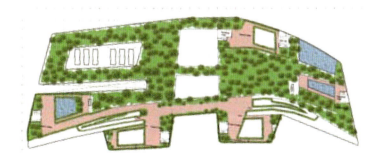

Level 5

Summary of Plans

Vertical Landscape Concept

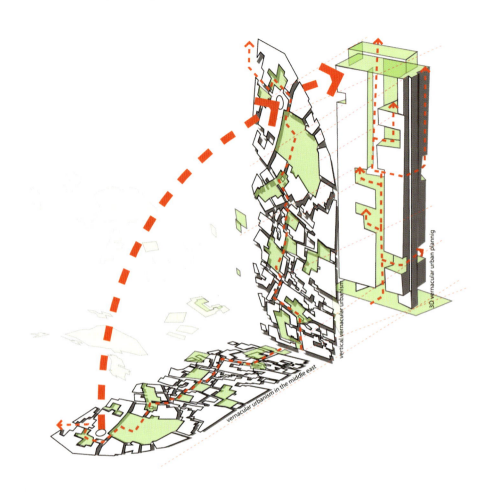

vertical vernacular urbanism

3D vernacular urban plannig

vernacular urbanism in the middle east

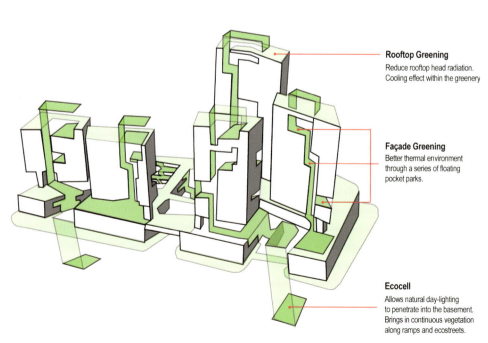

Rooftop Greening

Reduce rooftop head radiation.
Cooling effect within the greenery

Façade Greening

Better thermal environment
through a series of floating
pocket parks.

Ecocell

Allows natural day-lighting
to penetrate into the basement.
Brings in continuous vegetation
along ramps and ecostreets.

Aerial View

Atrium View

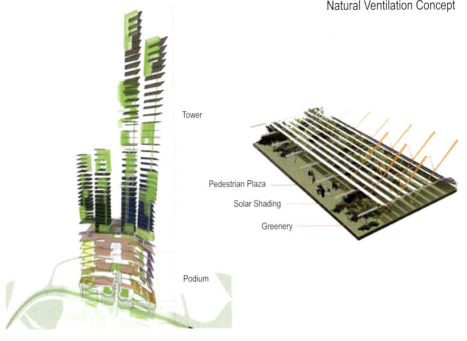

Tower

Pedestrian Plaza

Solar Shading

Greenery

Podium

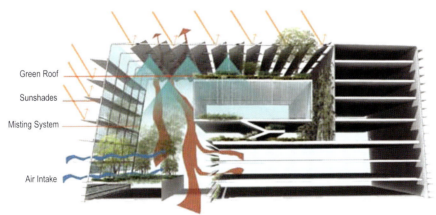

Green Roof

Sunshades

Misting System

Air Intake

Convection of Hot Air

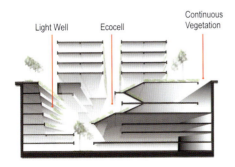

Light Well   Ecocell   Continuous Vegetation

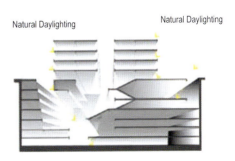

Natural Daylighting   Natural Daylighting

South Elevation

South View

Night View

KIA Tower

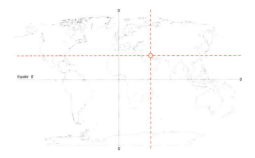

Location
Kuwait City, Kuwait

Climate Zone
Desert

Vegetation Zone
Semi Desert-Shrub

No. of Storeys
65

Areas
GFA   : 82,000 m²
NFA   : 57,000 m²

Site Area
11,837 m²

Plot Ratio
1:7

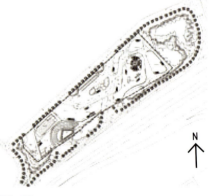

Site Plan

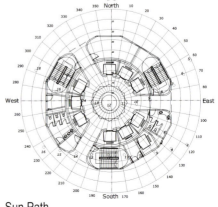

Sun Path

The KIA Tower design concept is derived from a desert flower to symbolise progress in a harsh desert environment. The idea is based on the shape of three petals spiralling 180 degrees to the top of the building. The three strands symbolise rapid growth in Kuwait's development, representing its culture, society and economy. The intertwining form emerges from the ground as if it has grown from the site. It will become an iconic building forming a landmark statement on the skyline of Kuwait city. The twisting forms of the building allow 360 degree views towards the sea, Kuwait city and the desert. Ecological design features are used to reduce running costs and overall impact on the environment. The tower incorporates passive mode skyscraper design, which suits the hot and arid climate. Intermediate sky courts create cool microclimates on the building's façades and integrated vegetation creates milder conditions within the building envelope. The main design features are expressed by the exoskeleton structure that defines the building's external façades. The continuation of the building's organic form is achieved via a spiraling effect from the vegetated landscaped podium up through spiraling sky courts. Ramping vegetation onto the podium creates roof gardens that become recreational spaces and contribute to a pleasant environment for occupants.

K
I
A

T
O
W
E
R

The design concept is based on a desert flower.

Aerial View

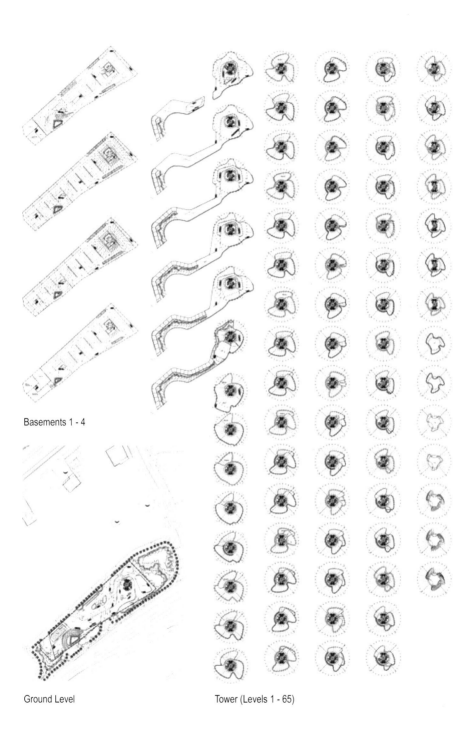

Basements 1 - 4

Ground Level

Tower (Levels 1 - 65)

N

Summary of Plans

South View

Ventilation Diagram

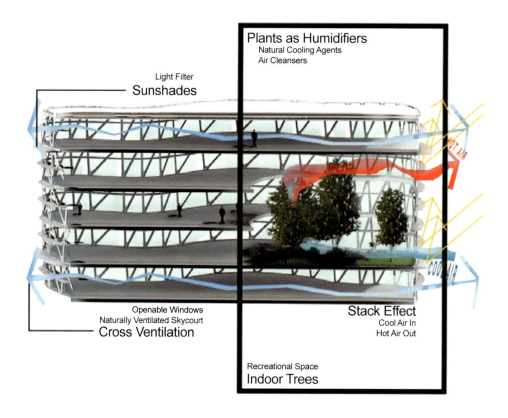

Plants as Humidifiers
Natural Cooling Agents
Air Cleansers

Light Filter
Sunshades

Stack Effect
Cool Air In
Hot Air Out

Openable Windows
Naturally Ventilated Skycourt
Cross Ventilation

Recreational Space
Indoor Trees

Ecocell Diagrams

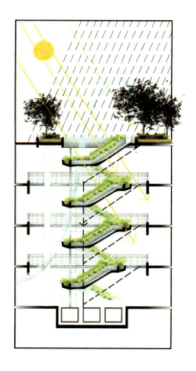

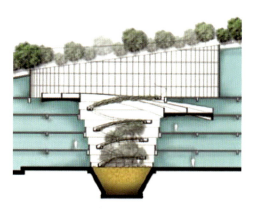

Ecological Features

Greywater Recycling
Rainwater Harvesting
Solar Photovoltaic Cells
Mixed-Mode Cooling
Motion-Sensor Controlled Lighting
Motorised Office Blinds
Extensive Sunshades
Water Conserving Landscaping
Water-Efficient Fixtures
Bioswales
Ecocells

Circulation

Circulation is enhanced by utilising high-tech vertical transportation such as express lifts, sky lobbies, services lifts and car parking lifts. Sky lobbies serve as transitional and communal spaces.

Floor Plans

The floor plan is derived to allow better views of the city and allow more individual floors for the building. Its curves allow each space to have panoramic views while the glass walls of internal lift lobbies maximise exterior views.

Podium

The ramping shape of the podium is sensitive towards the local low-rise context and serves as an ecological green lung for the building, enhancing the quality of its public spaces. Large span structures in the tower allow for maximum flexibility for internal layouts, which in turn creates higher quality spaces.

Sky Courts

Sky courts create lush environments for the people inside the building. Their recessed design shades offices from direct sunlight and reduces glare. Integrated landscaping reduces the ambient temperature of the building, increasing thermal comfort and the efficiency of engineering systems. Plants also act as visual screens and sound diffusers to reduce pollution from surrounding areas.

Roof

The rooftop serves as a viewing deck, the location of executive lounges and an area for functions and special occasions. It is an exclusive level and one of the centrepieces of the development.

Plaza of Nations

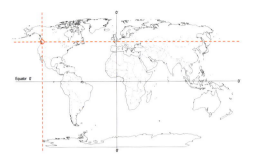

Location
Vancouver, Canada

Climate Zone
Temperate

Vegetation Zone
Mountainous Forest

No. of Storeys
64

Areas
GFA   : 300,000 m^2
NFA   : 246,000 m^2

Site Area
27,000 m^2

Plot Ratio
1:11

Site Plan

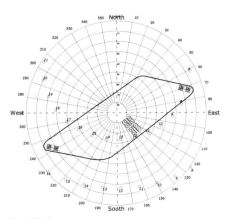

Sun Path

Location Plan

The vision for the Vancouver Waterfront site is to create an exemplary deep green development for the city of Vancouver that enriches our knowledge about sustainable communities, ecodensity and zero-carbon development. The proposed development comprises seven residential tower blocks, one hotel tower and three levels of commercial development. Civic facilities in the residential towers include daycare, community sky gardens, roof gardens and park spaces.

Ecologically, the design possesses a number of unique biodiversity features. These include: rooftop gardens on all towers; high-level ecobridges with vegetation that connect the towers; mid-level vegetated sky courts, with biomass continuing upwards on the towers' façades to the rooftop gardens; and the garden/park on the roof of the retail podium, accessible by vegetated ramps from the ground. Stepped planting systems are installed on every tower façade so that the vegetation is brought upwards to all floors from the ground. This integrates the inorganic mass of the built form with a natural organic mass by imitating the biotic structure of natural ecosystems.

Masterplan

The garden/park on the rooftop of the retail podium will form a landscaped zone that interconnects the project with its surrounding ecological context. Accessed via a network of ramps from Pacific Boulevard and the waterfront sea wall, this area will accommodate large trees and become a stunningly unique and attractive addition to the Vancouver skyline. A mixture of hardy shrub, perennial and grass species will provide ground cover and seasonal interest. These species have been selected to enhance the existing biodiversity of flora and fauna. The garden/ park will also afford magnificent views, both out to the waterfront and back to the city.

In terms of human infrastructure, the design is a new urban high-rise typology—one that is iconically and explicitly green. Its integration of built form with landscaped gardens, ramps and bridges-in-the-sky will showcase a new exemplary form for future eco-skyscrapers on Vancouver's skyline.

The development also displays a unique approach to urban design and public-realm place-making. Among its features are: publicly accessible function rooms at the uppermost floors of the two tallest towers; a lively central plaza at ground level in the retail podium, open to the sky and sweeping out to the waterfront, that will have programmed cultural, entertainment and trade events throughout the year; and secondary event spaces located along the waterfront and adjoining developments that will have similar programmed events and activities. The public realm has been conceived as a unifying feature that will contribute to the overall character of Vancouver's waterfront redevelopment. A variety of places will be provided to accommodate the needs of the vast number of people who live, work, pass through and visit the waterfront area.

False Creek Night View

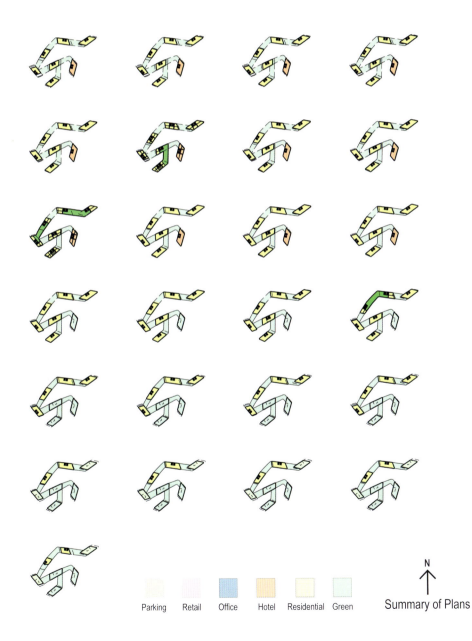

Parking   Retail   Office   Hotel   Residential   Green

Summary of Plans

N

Landscaped Podium

Entrance Plaza

False Creek Seawall

View from BC Place

False Creek Seawall View

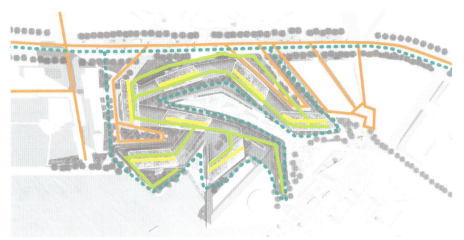

Circulation Diagram

Night View from False Creek

P Tower

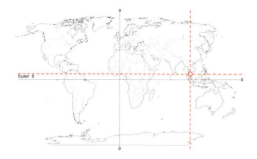

Location
Kuala Lumpur, Malaysia

Climate Zone
Tropical

Vegetation Zone
Rainforest

No. of Storeys
30

Areas
GFA   : 43,008 m²
NFA   : 34,370 m²

Site Area
5479 m²

Plot Ratio
1:8

Site Plan

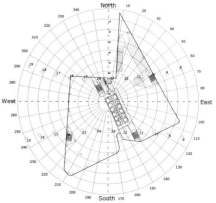

Sun Path

South View

The P Tower reflects a unique skyrise greenery design concept. Six large multi-storey sky gardens provide open spaces and green views for occupants of the upper levels of the building without compromising the overall efficiency of office floorplates. A series of internal ramps within these zones create escalating sequences of pocket parks and provide direct access to the gardens from multiple levels of adjacent offices. The gardens are designed to accomodate office ammenities such as food courts, dry-cleaners, convenience stores, childcare centres and medical clinics. The sky gardens are also positioned to capitalise on subsequent revisions to local zoning ordinances by allowing additional floor area to be seamlessly phased into the development at a later date. Water for the irrigation of all vegetated areas within the building is provided via a rainwater harvesting system located at the basement and rooftop levels.

Continuous bands of sunshade louvres on the building's external façades help reduce solar heat gain and maintain comfortable thermal conditions within the naturally ventilated gardens. The walls of the tower's central elevator core are clad with a modular vertical green-wall system that extends continuously from the ground level to the highest roof garden.

The P Tower's incorporation of ground level landscaping, roof gardens, green walls and extensive sky gardens produces a formidable vision of urban ecology. The project's overall landscaped areas exceed its site area by nearly 300%. In contrast to typical urban developments in which natural landscapes are subverted or paved over, the P Tower is designed to both enhance and increase the ecological footprint of its urban site.

P

T
O
W
E
R

South Elevation

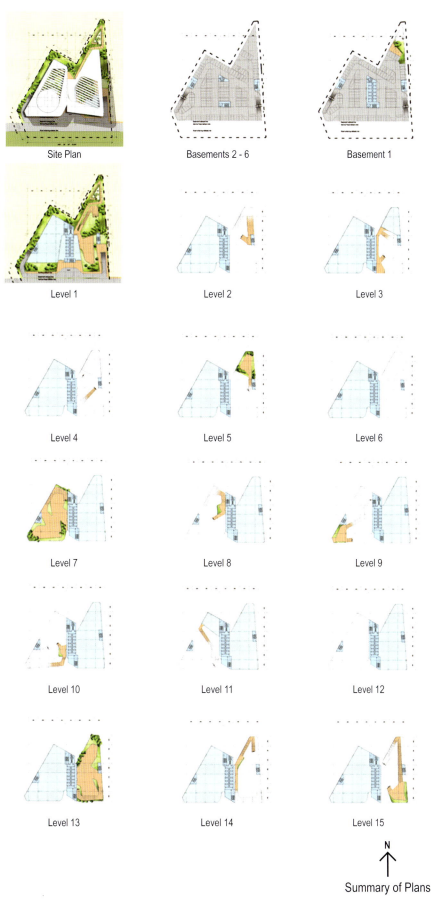

Site Plan

Basements 2 - 6

Basement 1

Level 1

Level 2

Level 3

Level 4

Level 5

Level 6

Level 7

Level 8

Level 9

Level 10

Level 11

Level 12

Level 13

Level 14

Level 15

P
T
O
W
E
R

N

Summary of Plans

Office
Office
Office
Office
Office
Office

Office
Office
Office
Office
Office
Office

Office
Office
Office
Office
Office

Office
Office
Office
Office
Office
Office

Office
Office
Office
Office

Lobby

Car Park
Car Park
Car Park
Car Park
Car Park

Car Park
Car Park
Car Park
Car Park
Car Park

Section

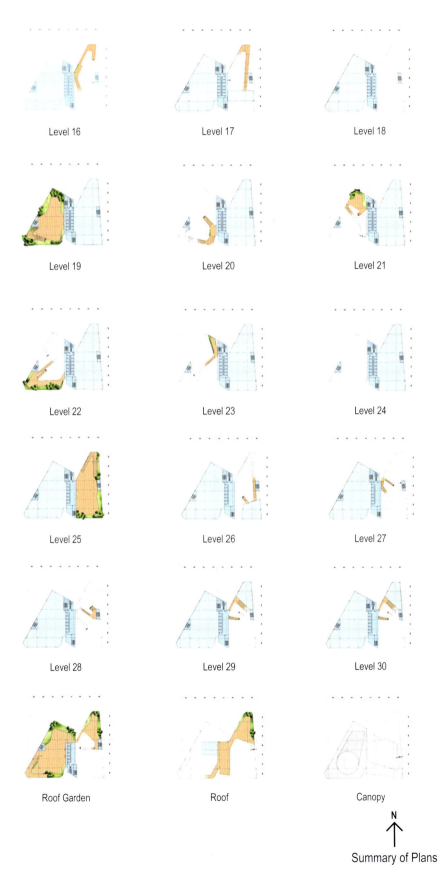

Level 16

Level 17

Level 18

Level 19

Level 20

Level 21

Level 22

Level 23

Level 24

Level 25

Level 26

Level 27

Level 28

Level 29

Level 30

Roof Garden

Roof

Canopy

P
T
O
W
E
R

N

Summary of Plans

Sunshade Louvre Concept

Sky Terrace Concept

Office Floor Concept

Building Envelope

Shenzhen Garden City

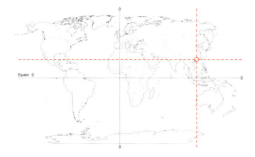

Location
Shenzhen, China

Climate Zone
Tropical

Vegetation Zone
Forest

No. of Storeys
39

Areas
GFA   : 274,305 m^2
NFA   : 249,745 m^2

Site Area
48,661 m^2

Plot Ratio
1:6

Site Plan

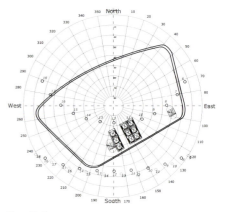

Sun Path

The Shenzhen Garden City reflects a state-of-the-art, high-tech, deep green design. Its unique design integrates nature with human life, bonded together with sustainable ecoengineering, creating a pleasurable and high quality environment for the project's inhabitants.

The development's dominant design feature is a leisure park that serves residents at the podium level. The activities and facilities at this level are linked to vertical sky forests, new densely planted vegetation that extends up the residential and office towers and interconnects with each of the project's landscaped areas. This Urban Forest on the podium roof enhances the aesthetic of the development and provides a framework for the project's sustainable water engineering systems.

Ecological Concept

Central Fountain View

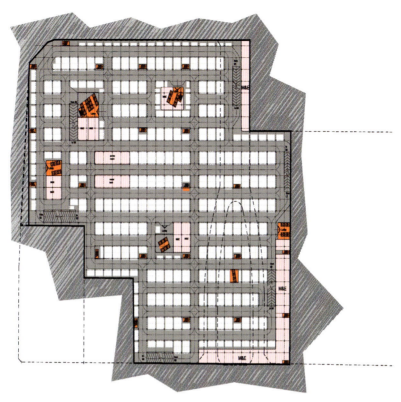

Basement 2

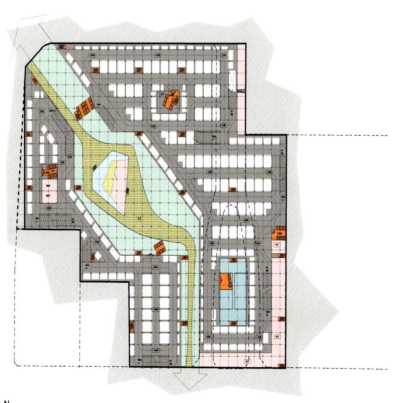

Basement 1

N

Summary of Plans

Urban Forest View

The Urban Forest is lifted off the ground level to allow vehicular traffic to pass through underneath. This design reduces the impact of traffic noise and pollution on the users of the development. The undulating topography of this level also creates various possibilities for indoor/outdoor activities on this level.

Ground Level

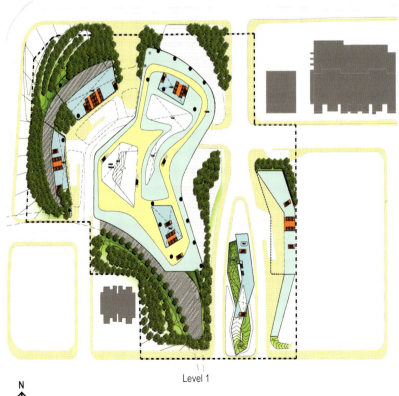

Level 1

N

Summary of Plans

Sky Link View

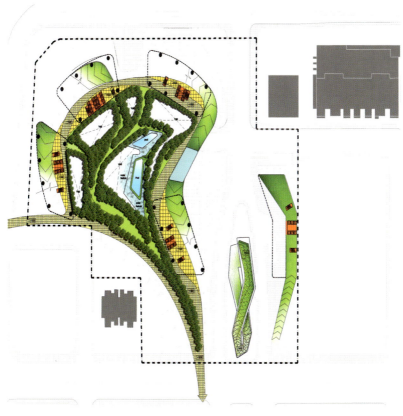

Level 2

N

Summary of Plans

Level 3

Residential Tower Elevations

DB Tower

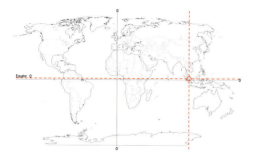

Location
Johor Bahru, Malaysia

Climate Zone
Tropical

Vegetation Zone
Rainforest

No. of Storeys
12

Areas
GFA   : 12,254 m²
NFA   : 9,494 m²

Site Area
3504 m²

Plot Ratio
1:3.5

Site Plan

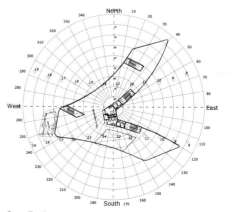

Sun Path

The DB Tower is an office and boutique hotel development in Johor Bahru, Malaysia. The project comprises a 12-storey tower located along a waterfront promenade and marina complex. The mixed-use tower combines offices, showrooms and a 150-room boutique hotel.

The tower's dynamic, futuristic form is shaped to maximise views of the waterfront. Each hotel room is angled to take advantage of sweeping ocean views. The resulting floor plan resembles the shape of the Chinese character 'ren', meaning 'people', as indeed the building is designed with people in mind.

The massing of the tower is interspersed with generous vegetated terraces at various floor intervals. These landscaped gardens balance the inorganic components of the development, bringing greenery into the upper levels of the building for the enjoyment of the guests and users. The greenery looks spectacular against the magnificent waterfront backdrop.

DB

TOWER

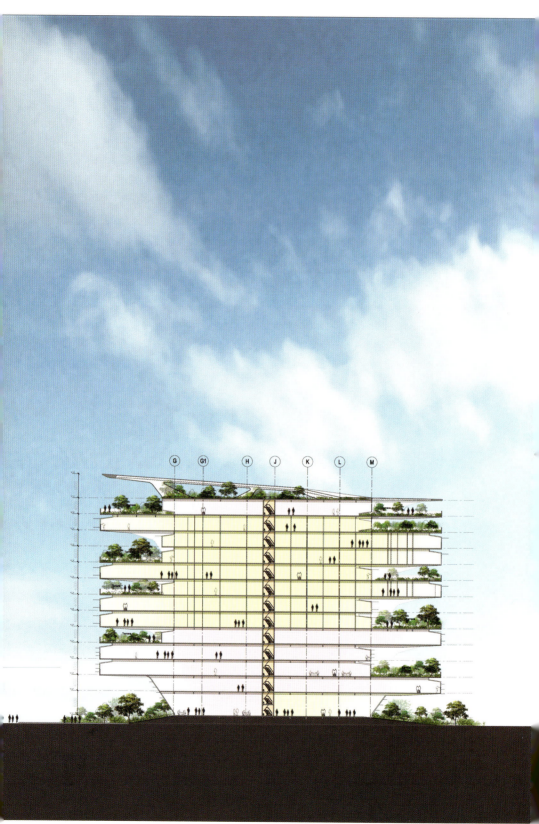

Section

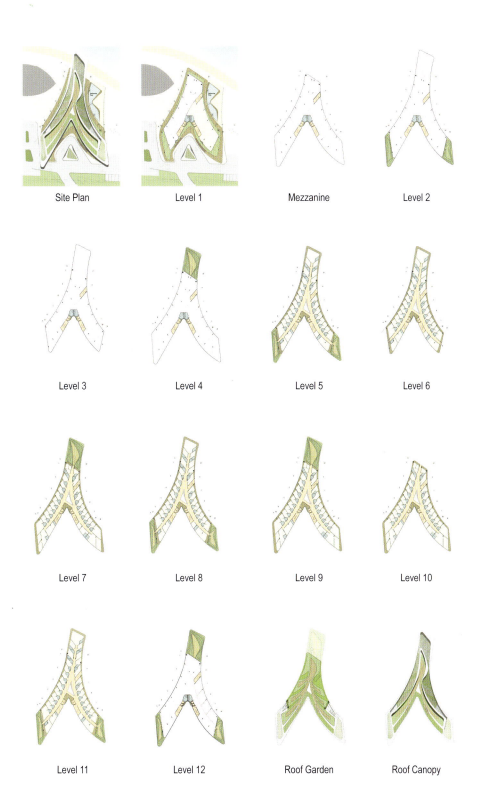

Site Plan

Level 1

Mezzanine

Level 2

Level 3

Level 4

Level 5

Level 6

Level 7

Level 8

Level 9

Level 10

Level 11

Level 12

Roof Garden

Roof Canopy

D
B

T
O
W
E
R

Summary of Plans

Beach Promenade View

Entrance View

G Tower

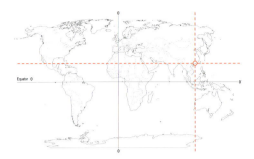

Location
Shenzhen, China

Climate Zone
Tropical

Vegetation Zone
Forest

No. of Storeys
47

Areas
GFA   : 77,408 m^2
NFA   : 57,028 m^2

Site Area
5455 m^2

Plot Ratio
1:14.7

Site Plan

N

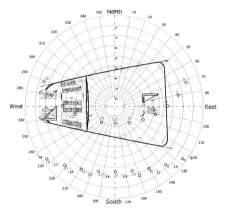

Sun Path

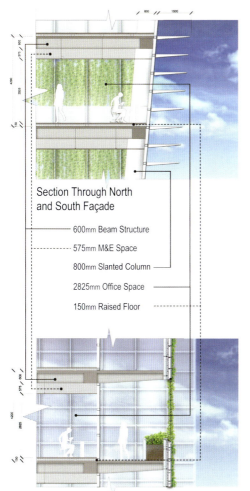

Section Through North
and South Façade

600mm Beam Structure

575mm M&E Space

800mm Slanted Column

2825mm Office Space

150mm Raised Floor

Section Through East and West Façade

The design of the G Tower at Shenzhen, China uniquely integrates nature with human living, bonded together with sustainable cleantech ecoengineering, creating diverse and pleasant workspaces-in-the-sky. Very high quality environments are provided for the people who use the built spaces and facilities. The project employs the latest ecotechnologies including ground source heat pumps, energy-efficient light systems, sustainable drainage and water management systems, recycling and rainwater harvesting, low-energy HVAC systems, low consumption appliances and building integrated photovoltaics.

To create a symbiotic balance between nature and the built environment, the tower incorporates the latest technology of vertical green-wall systems to act as a biodiverse smart skin for the façade. This purifies air before it enters interior spaces. The impact of morning and evening solar heat gain is mitigated via a combination of modular and trellised green-wall systems. These systems shade the building's façade, create occupiable microclimates on external landscaped terraces and facilitate natural ventilation in common areas and the tower's cores.

Various sky courts, sky meeting rooms and roof gardens are created to provide diverse and interactive spaces for the building's users. The flexibility of these spaces not only fulfils the functionality of the client's brief, but also provides areas that enhance wellbeing and quality of life. These sky rooms host within them different user areas, such as breakout spaces, meeting spaces, relaxation spaces, meditation, reading and quiet spaces. They also bring the pleasantness of the green environment from the ground into upper parts of the building for the benefit of its users.

G
T
O
W
E
R

Eye-Level View

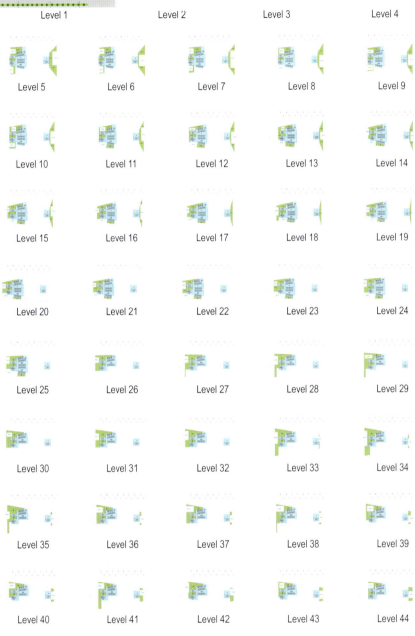

Level 1 Level 2 Level 3 Level 4

Level 5 Level 6 Level 7 Level 8 Level 9

Level 10 Level 11 Level 12 Level 13 Level 14

Level 15 Level 16 Level 17 Level 18 Level 19

Level 20 Level 21 Level 22 Level 23 Level 24

Level 25 Level 26 Level 27 Level 28 Level 29

Level 30 Level 31 Level 32 Level 33 Level 34

Level 35 Level 36 Level 37 Level 38 Level 39

Level 40 Level 41 Level 42 Level 43 Level 44

Level 45 Level 46 Level 47

G
T
O
W
E
R

N

Summary of Plans

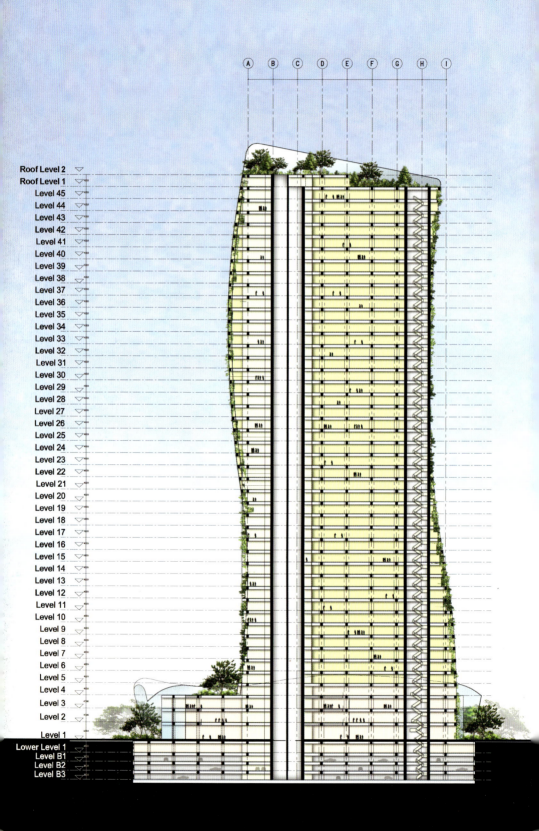

Roof Level 2
Roof Level 1
Level 45
Level 44
Level 43
Level 42
Level 41
Level 40
Level 39
Level 38
Level 37
Level 36
Level 35
Level 34
Level 33
Level 32
Level 31
Level 30
Level 29
Level 28
Level 27
Level 26
Level 25
Level 24
Level 23
Level 22
Level 21
Level 20
Level 19
Level 18
Level 17
Level 16
Level 15
Level 14
Level 13
Level 12
Level 11
Level 10
Level 9
Level 8
Level 7
Level 6
Level 5
Level 4
Level 3
Level 2
Level 1
Lower Level 1
Level B1
Level B2
Level B3

A B C D E F G H I

Section

Night View

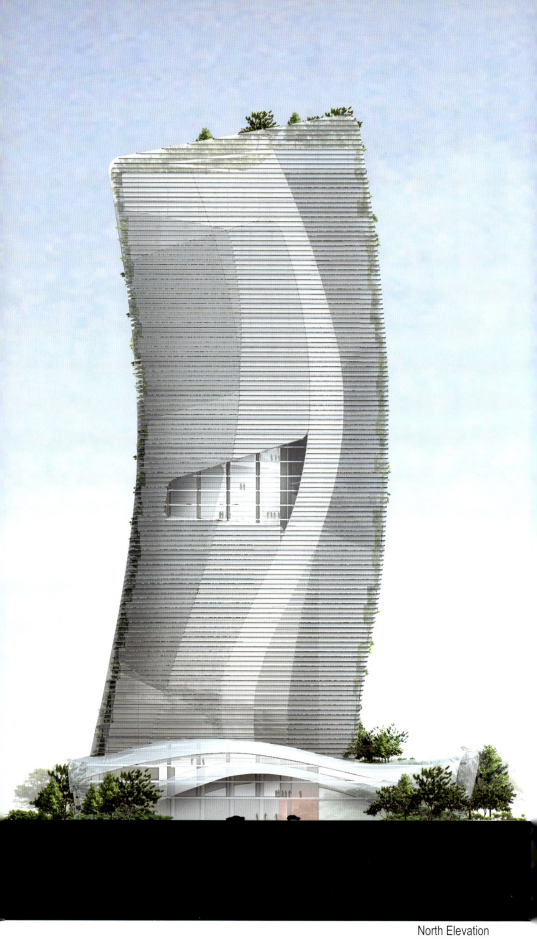

North Elevation

West Elevation

Entrance View

Ecological Concept

Rooftop Garden

Vertical Green Wall

Skycourts

Urban Garden

Surrounding Green

Rainwater Harvesting System

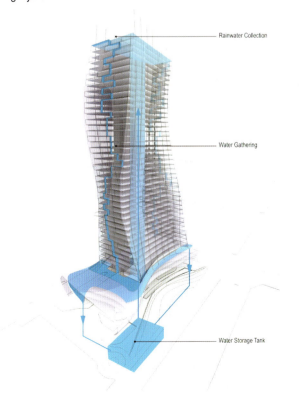

Rainwater Collection

Water Gathering

Water Storage Tank

EcoInfrastructure Diagrams

A holistic green design is created by weaving four infrastructures into a whole.

Red Infrastructure

 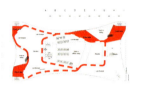 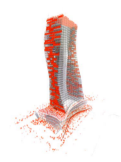

Level 1
Continuous Walkway and Public Plazas

Level 4 Sky Garden
Continuous Walkway and Public Plazas

Green Infrastructure

  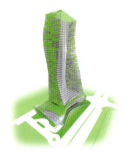

Level 1
Green Space and Garden

Level 4 Sky Garden
Green Space and Garden

Grey Infrastructure

Basement 1
M&E Space

Typical Floor
M&E Space

Blue Infrastructure

Basement 1, 2 and 3
Water Storage Tank

Aerial Perspective

Acknowledgements

I am delighted to acknowledge Alessina Brooks and Paul Latham for their continued support and help in the dissemination of our ideas. I also wish to thank Debbie Fry at Images Publishing for her guidance and editing of this book.

I am indebted to Mitch Gelber for his many contributions to our Kuala Lumpur office over the past three years. He has been instrumental in designing, writing and project managing this volume with the support of our designer, Hafiz Shah.

I am grateful to Lord Norman Foster of Riverside for his very kind support of my ideas and work. I am also very grateful to all those who have taught me over the years and have given their incisive comments to advance the work and ideas, in particular Professor John Frazer (Queensland University of Technology), Professor Alan Balfour (Georgia Tech, Atlanta), Professor Jeffrey Kipnis (The Ohio State University), Professor Mohsen Mostafavi (Harvard Graduate School of Design), and others, too numerous to mention.